Niagara Falls

Niagara Falls

by

Dirk Vanderwilt

Niagara Falls, 3rd Edition (*Tourist Town Guides*®)
© 2010 by Dirk Vanderwilt

Published by:
Channel Lake, Inc., P.O. Box 1771, New York, NY 10156-1771
http://www.channellake.com

Author: Dirk Vanderwilt
Editorial and Page Layout: Quadrum Solutions (http://www.quadrumltd.com)
Cover Design: Julianna Lee
Front Cover Photos:
"Maid of the Mist" © Dirk Vanderwilt
"Skylon Tower" © iStockphoto.com/mikedabell
"American Falls" © iStockphoto.com/CaptainIFR
Back Cover Photo:
"Rapids" © Dirk Vanderwilt

Published in April, 2010

ISBN: 978-1-935455-03-5

Disclaimer: The information in this book has been checked for accuracy. However, neither the publisher nor the author may be held liable for errors or omissions. *Use this book at your own risk.* To obtain the latest information, we recommend that you contact the vendors directly. If you do find an error, let us know at corrections@channellake.com

Channel Lake, Inc. is not affiliated with the vendors mentioned in this book, and the vendors have not authorized, approved or endorsed the information contained herein. This book contains the opinions of the author, and your experience may vary.

For more information, visit http://www.touristtown.com

Help Our Environment!

Even when on vacation, your responsibility to protect the environment does not end. Here are some ways you can help our planet without spoiling your fun:

★ Ask your hotel staff not to clean your towels and bed linens each day. This reduces water waste and detergent pollution.

★ Turn off the lights, heater, and/or air conditioner when you leave your hotel room, and keep that thermostat low!

★ Use public transportation when available. Tourist trolleys are very popular, and they are usually cheaper and easier than a car.

★ Recycle everything you can, and properly dispose of rubbish in labeled receptacles.

Tourist towns consume a lot of energy. Have fun, but don't be wasteful. Please do your part to ensure that these attractions are around for future generations to visit and enjoy.

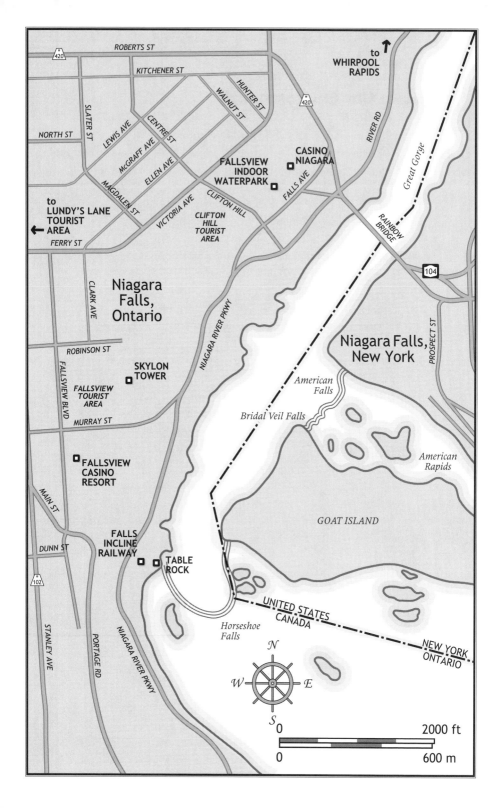

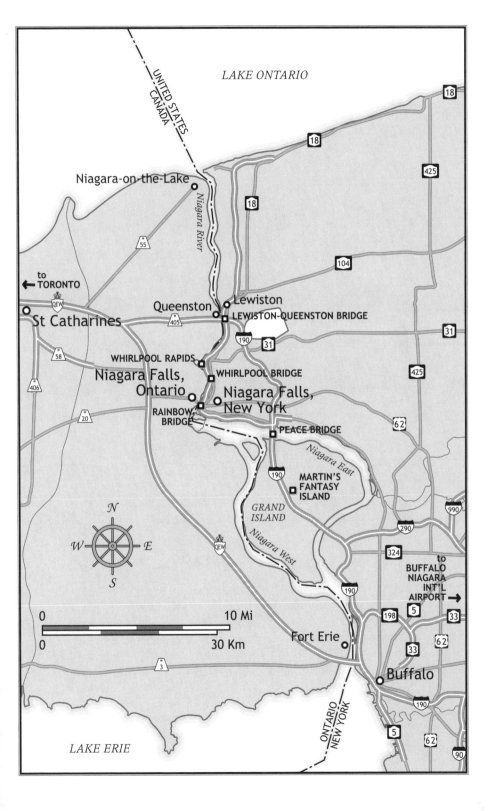

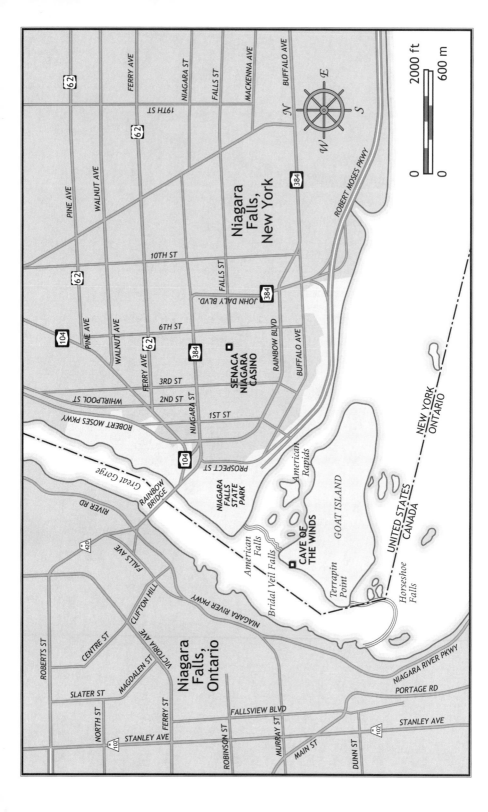

Table of Contents

How to Use this Book

Tourist Town Guides® makes it easy to find exactly what you are looking for! Just flip to a chapter or section that interests you. The tabs on the margins will help you find your way quickly.

Attractions are usually listed by subject groups. Attractions may have an address, Web site (🖱), and/or telephone number (☎) listed.

Must-See Attractions: Headlining must-see attractions, or those that are otherwise iconic or defining, are designated with the ⭐ Must See! symbol.

Coverage: This book is not all-inclusive. It is comprehensive, with many different options for entertainment, dining, shopping, etc. but there are many establishments not listed here.

Prices: At the end of many attraction listings is a general pricing reference, indicated by dollar signs, relative to other attractions in the region. The scale is from "$" (least expensive) to "$$$" (most expensive). Contact the attraction directly for specific pricing information.

Niagara Falls was formed about 12,000 years ago, but they looked very different back then. And it was not located in the same place along the Niagara River.

Introduction

"The mass of water, striking some ever-hidden base of rock, leaps up the whole two hundred feet again in pinnacles and domes of spray. The spray falls back into the lower river once more; all but a little that fines to foam and white mist, which drifts in layers along the air, graining it, and wanders out on the wind over the trees and gardens and houses, and so vanishes..."

– Rupert Brooke, on Horseshoe Falls, 1913

Niagara Falls is a place with many faces. Its numerous resort-hotels and breathtaking scenery make it a romantic retreat. The museums, video arcades, and sideshows make it a popular family destination. The area's hiking and wilderness trails make it perfect for nature lovers. And yet, despite all the secondary distractions, the falls themselves have managed to avoid being overshadowed. They are powerful, beautiful, and awe-inspiring. They demand attention. They demand to be at the forefront. It is oftentimes difficult to believe that such a unique natural wonder exists so near America's east coast.

The Niagara River connects two of the American Great Lakes: Lake Erie in the south and Lake Ontario in the north. The Niagara Escarpment cuts right through the river, drastically changing the height of the water in only a few short feet. Thus, the water on the Niagara River must "fall" to reach the river as the elevation drops along the escarpment. The elevation difference is the primary factor in determining that the water flows north – Lake Ontario is lower than Lake Erie.

The falls are also politically interesting. They are shared between two countries, the United States and Canada. Each country claims a portion of the falls to be its own, and each country vies for tourist dollars in different ways. Both cities are named Niagara Falls. But these cities are independent of each other, with individual governments, in individual nations. Though they have some agreements, they are largely – and obviously – quite different in character.

Horseshoe Falls, Bridal Veil Falls, and American Falls – which together form the "Niagara Falls" we know today, are products of the ice age, as was the entire Great Lakes region. The falls have been flowing for about 12,000 years. But they are not stationary. In fact, they have been moving south, up the Niagara River, slowly grinding away at the rocks. They have been moving and will continue to move until the waters stops flowing.

Visitors come in droves – over 14 million each year – to see some of the most impressive waterfalls in America. When gazed upon for the first time, the falls are simply breathtaking.

But in today's society, there is only so much time that we can spend staring at water falling. They may glance at them and take photos of them; they may even take a boat ride up close to them. But where do they go afterwards? What's next? What can millions of people who visit each year do in Niagara Falls?

Niagara Falls History

During the most recent ice age, a huge ice sheet covered most of Canada and parts of the northern United States (including New York and Chicago). Called the Laurentide ice sheet, it was about one to two miles thick, and hundreds of thousands of miles long. For about 70,000 years it sat, occasionally growing and receding, but by far the dominant feature and influence of the landscape and climate. But around 18,000 years ago, the age began to wind down, climate shifted, and the ice sheet started to shrink.

THE GREAT LAKES REGION

The receding Laurentide ice sheet greatly shaped the ecology and geography of some of the northern United States and much of Canada. The melting ice carved holes, redirected rivers, and dumped countless gallons of water onto the continent. The most significant of these was Lake Agassiz. Located in the center of North America, the lake was much bigger than all the Great Lakes combined, and it spanned about 440,000 square miles. Laurentide fed the lake as it melted, and it was overflowing. So the fresh water was spilling all over the place; creating and filling new rivers and lakes. The overflowing water eventually made its way to the other large holes left by the ice sheet – about 12,000 years ago, the holes were filled, and the Great Lakes were born. Eventually, Laurentide vanished completely, Agassiz's water source was gone, and over the next 1,000 years, the lake drained completely.

Partly in the northern United States and partly in southern Canada, the newly formed five Great Lakes are the largest collection of freshwater lakes in the world. They are, from west to east: Lake Superior, Lake Michigan, Lake Huron, Lake Erie, and Lake Ontario. Each lake is connected by a natural system of waterways; these lakes and the fact that they connect to each other would become fundamental in the economic development of the region. (A sixth, much smaller lake, Lake St. Clair, is part of the same system of waterways, but is not considered an official "Great Lake.")

FORMATION OF NIAGARA FALLS

The Niagara River is about 35 miles long and connects Lake Erie to Lake Ontario. If it weren't for the Niagara Escarpment – a stretch of elevated rock that encircles the eastern section of the Great Lakes region, there would not be much to tell about this river. However, the escarpment cuts right through it, causing a sudden shift in elevation. The water drops about 170 feet (only 70 feet if the rocks at the base of the falls are considered). Thus, it is not a very high waterfall, but it is exceptionally wide, with over 150,000 gallons of water per second flowing over the edge (the largest amount by far in America). In total, the elevation of the Niagara River drops about 330 feet along its path from Erie to Ontario. Most of the feeding waters of Niagara Falls, mainly from Lake Erie, are directly from the ice sheet, which are not replenished.

The falls themselves were born about 12,000 years ago, along with the Niagara River and various area waterways and lakes. There were originally five smaller waterfalls, which were eventually combined into one. The one large fall started its journey along the Niagara River at Queenston and Lewiston, over four miles north of its current location. From there, the constant running of water has been grinding into the bedrock, moving the falls slowly upstream.

But the falls stalled about 7,000 years later, when Lake Erie's waters stopped feeding the river. For various geological reasons, the flow of the falls was reduced to a mere ten percent, and for the next 5,000 years, it stood almost stagnant. When normal flow resumed, it continued its path up the river.

Years later, as the falls continued carving into Lake Erie, they uncovered a large underground river. In a sudden burst that lasted only a few days, the seal of this river was broken open, which destroyed the falls and turned them into a series of steep rapids. In the course of only a few short weeks, the falls made a sharp 90-degree turn and continued the path, eventually re-establishing itself as a waterfall. The remnants of this event is today called the Whirlpool Rapids – the largest collection of standing waves in the country.

There, the falls continue to make slow progress to their ultimate destination – Lake Ontario. However, gradual erosion has been greatly reduced because of modern human intervention. Today, the amount of water passing through Niagara Falls is tightly controlled. A power plant, which has the capacity to divert most of the water away from the falls, regulates the flow, which changes seasonally and even daily, depending on power needs and other factors. The flow is reduced when the plant diverts more water. In an emergency, operators have the capability to minimize the flow over the brink.

However, on March 28, 1869, the flow to all the falls was stopped completely for a few hours, because of an iceberg blocking water flow upstream. Additionally, in 1969, the

American Falls was intentionally stopped for several months. At the time, they were trying to remove some rocks from the base. It was deemed unfeasibly expensive.

EARLY SETTLERS AND EXPLORATION

The first known human inhabitants of the Niagara Falls were wanderers known as the Clovis people. Near the end of the ice age, about 12,000 years ago, these hunter-gatherers would live in tiny settlements near the edge of Lake Erie. They would hunt local animals, such as caribou and moose. At this time, the falls were just beginning to form as the ice slowly melted.

Over many generations, different peoples would make their way through the region, stopping for only a time around the river. The land was cold; with a landscape consisting of forests of spruce, which were capable of surviving in the harsh tundra environment. As the environment warmed a deciduous forest rose, covering much of the area. Eventually the Iroquois Native Americans made much of southern Ontario their home and stayed there for many centuries. By the 1500s, the Iroquois nations were complex, with complete political and economic (trading) systems in place. They called the river – a primary source of water for settlements in the area –"Onguiaahra," which means "the strait."

Eventually, however, wars broke out among the Iroquois nations, particularly the five in New York State. The Niagara region became hostile, and the new European explorations of the area did not help matters. In the 1500s–1600s, explorers began to scope out the land, including Jacques Cartier and Samuel De Champlain. It wasn't until around 1615 that the first European explorer, Etienne Brule, saw the falls. The first record of the river's name was by a Jesuit Priest – who "simplified" the Iroquois name into simply "Niagara." Despite the onslaught of European explorers, the Iroquois managed to keep western settlement from occupying the region until the American Revolution, over 100 years later.

The United States declared war on the British in 1812. This war, fought on American soil, had the U.S. fighting mainly Canadian militia – since Canada was under British rule at the time. Called the "second war of independence," the United States was able to stave off the British for a second time, even though much of the fighting was done between Canada and the U.S.

After two years, when the war was over, the Niagara region was badly damaged.

TRANSPORTATION DEVELOPMENT

Niagara has an extensive transportation history – the modern eras of Ontario, New York, and the Great Lakes region were largely the result of transport through this region, so traffic and trade was always busy, and it got busier.

With the lakes allowing commercial trade to travel as far inland as Lake Superior, it was thought that the development of navigable waterways was essential (to allow sea-going vessels passage to over a thousand miles inland). However, the waterways connecting the lakes posed many problems. Rapids, waterfalls, power dams, and other natural and man-made obstacles made it impossible for ships to make the passage. Therefore, over time, a series of connecting waterways were created. Built in the 1800s and early 1900s and called the Saint

Lawrence Seaway and Great Lakes Waterway, these canals consisted of a series of locks that allowed vessels to bypass these obstacles. Among them, the Welland Canal, connecting Lake Ontario to Lake Erie, bypasses Niagara Falls. To complete the transport path, connecting the Great Lakes to the Atlantic Ocean is the Erie Canal. This man-made waterway connects Lake Erie to the Hudson River, which in turn flows directly into the Atlantic.

The Niagara River had its share of transportation booms as well. Ferry transportation service began to cross the river downstream of the falls in the mid-1820s. Later that decade, a paved road was built to the ferry landing (on the Canadian side), which ran through the tiny settlement of Clifton – where hotels and other commercial services began to spring up. Between the late 1800s and early 1900s, 13 bridges were built crossing the Niagara River. One of these was the Niagara Railway Suspension Bridge, conceived by John Roebling (the Brooklyn Bridge architect).

THE UNDERGROUND RAILROAD

For almost as long as there was slavery in the United States, there was the Underground Railroad. Using railroad terminology as a code, this secret network of abolitionists and sympathetic souls helped thousands of men and women along their arduous journeys to freedom, oftentimes north to Canada. By the time slavery was abolished in 1865, the route taken by the fugitives, although always dangerous, was well established.

After a perilous trip across New York State, slaves would eventually arrive at the Niagara River. Crossing at certain "safe" locations along the river, the last leg of their journey took them from their status as slaves in the U.S. to free men and women in Canada. Niagara Falls, the nearby city of St. Catharine, and the entire Canadian Niagara region all served as final stops on the railroad. Countless people made this journey, and the Niagara region is full of reminders of this historical passage to freedom.

THE WAR OF 1812

Sometimes called the British-American War, the War of 1812 was very important in establishing Canada as an independent nation. Although they "officially" weren't involved in it, the country's militia fought the war on their soil.

After declaring independence from Great Britain in 1776, and following the American Revolutionary War, the United States had an uneasy relationship with the British, and relations were often strained. This came to a head on June 18, 1812, when the U.S. declared war on Great Britain for a variety of reasons: among others shipping embargos and agreements between Great Britain and France. The war was fought on Canadian and United States soil, so although the war was between the U.S. and the British, about half of the British fighters were Canadian. The war officially ended in 1815.

The war ended in a stalemate. The U.S. suffered more losses than Britain, whose involvement in the war ended up being only a minute detail. The real beneficiary of the war was Canada: The ability of the nation to protect itself against the U.S. attacks solidified Canada's status as a distinct nation, and many regard the Battle of Queenston Heights – arguably the most important battle of the war, where Canada's victory was immense – to be the "birth of Canada."

Today in the entire region there are numerous monuments and references to this war, including forts, monuments, and historic battlegrounds.

POWER IN NIAGARA

The Niagara River drops about 300 feet during its journey from Lake Erie to Lake Ontario. Most of that elevation drop occurs around the falls and whirlpool area. In fact, the water drops 71 feet from the base of Horseshoe Falls to the Whirlpool Rapids – a trip of only a few short miles. The energy-generation potential for this immense amount of falling water is no secret. It was first utilized in 1759 to power a nearby sawmill. Since then, more and more of the water had been used for greater and greater power.

At the dawn of commercial power consumption (around the 1870s–80s), it was the battle of direct versus alternating current. Thomas Edison had favored direct current, and was at the time promoting and distributing it. An additional and more flexible kind of power, the alternating current, was under development.

Using the Niagara River as a test bed, scientist Nikola Tesla built upon his knowledge of the alternating current and created the first commercially viable method of AC power; power that could be harnessed hydroelectrically and distributed to great distances. Later, inventor George Westinghouse was able to further modify Tesla's original concept, and in 1883 he lit the falls at night entirely with the new AC development.

Today, the flow of water over Niagara Falls – and particularly Horseshoe Falls – is tightly regulated to meet the needs of the area's power consumption and the tourist seasons. When water is used for power, it is diverted from the falls and passed through underground tunnels where the potential energy of the water drop is used to create power. Thus, the more water diverted, the less going over the falls (and less for the tourists to see). It is a fragile balance. In fact, about a quarter of the energy used to power New York State and Ontario comes directly from the hydroelectric plants on both the Canadian and American sides of the falls.

There are literally dozens of power generators along the Niagara River on both sides of the falls. Altogether, these hydroelectric plants generate as much as 4.4 kilowatts of power.

TOURISM

Commercial tourism to Niagara Falls began in the early 1820s, when the paved road brought travelers up from the newly built ferry landing at Table Rock to the settlement of Clifton, where hotels and commercial services would draw the crowds in. Although various peoples had visited Niagara Falls for thousands of years, it had not become much of a "tourist attraction" until the ferries and paved roads around the falls and Clifton made the area more accessible for westerners. At first, they would come to see the falls. They would spend the day on the edges of the Great Gorge, admiring the natural wonder that had befallen them. Occasionally, stunt performers would entertain them.

The first attraction in the area that was not directly related to the falls themselves became known as the **Burning Spring**. It was discovered, in as early as 1820, that a natural gas leak on what is now Dufferin Islands could be lit, and cause a rather unusual but controlled "natural gas fire." A building was built around it, and people would be allowed – for a price – to see the flame. The attraction is not there anymore, since **Queen Victoria Park** was created.

ICE BRIDGES

Niagara Falls does not freeze over, nor does the Niagara River. Even in the dead of winter, during the coldest months, there is always water flowing over the falls and north to Lake Ontario. However, because of a certain natural occurrence, the river immediately downstream of Niagara Falls sometimes gives the appearance of being frozen. This is called an "ice bridge."

Ice bridges form because chunks of ice, slush, and other forms of frozen water make their way from Erie, and then topple over Niagara Falls. The ice then floats a little bit downstream, but it eventually gets jammed. When lots of ice and slush chunks get pushed together, combined with the freezing temperatures, the chunks freeze together and form a bridge, connecting both sides of the river. Thus, it is an "ice bridge" because the Niagara River is still flowing swiftly underneath the surface of the ice.

Sometimes this ice bridge can extend to over a mile, and as much as 50 feet deep. It can last for only a few weeks or from as long as December to April. The bridge forms during most years, but it is never exactly the same. Sometimes, during the warmest winters, there is no ice bridge at all.

The ice bridge had been a popular pathway for tourists to walk upon, but it really became a booming attraction sometime in the 1840s. Gatherings would occur, merchants would sell their wares, and winter sporting activity would all take place on the ice. However, these activities were done with caution, because nobody could predict exactly how long each seasonal ice bridge would last.

In 1912, the unfortunate happened: the ice bridge of the season broke up unexpectedly and carried three tourists downriver, to their deaths. Since then, the ice bridge has been deemed unsafe and access is not allowed.

THE DUMPING SCOW

On August 6, 1918, a dumping scow was stranded in the upper Horseshoe Rapids after a failed attempt to drag it out of harm's way. Luckily all the passengers survived, but the ship was left in the river. It is still there today, a few hundred feet back from the falls.

NIAGARA "MIRACLES"

There have been only a few recorded cases of people surviving unaided plunges over Horseshoe Falls. Perhaps the most famous: In 1960, a pleasure boat upstream of the falls carried the Woodwards, a family of three. Their boat capsized. They drifted helplessly, and capsized a few hundred feet from the brink of Horseshoe Falls. The father, Jim, and the boat went over Horseshoe Falls. The father died. The two children, 17-year-old Deanne and 7-year-old Roger, drifted towards the falls wearing only life preservers. Miraculously, a tourist rescued the girl at Terrapin Point. But the young boy, Roger Woodward, sank underwater as he toppled helplessly over Horseshoe Falls.

During a regular tour, a **Maid of the Mist** tourist boat happened to see the floating life preserver by the base of the falls, and threw a rope out. Roger Woodward had survived the plunge.

DAREDEVILS AND STUNTS

Sometimes, simply admiring the falls from afar just isn't good enough. Some people want to "experience" them first hand. Maybe it's the possibility of fame. Maybe it's the thrill of the moment. Maybe it is just boredom with the everyday. Or maybe, it's just because it is there to conquer.

One of the first stunt performers was Sam Patch, who would jump into the Niagara River from a pre-built platform (not into the falls). The most famous early performer, however, was Jean Francois Gravelet, known professionally as Blondin. During two summers, one in 1850 and one in 1859, on a tightrope over the Great Gorge, a safe distance from the falls, he would perform all kinds of acts for crowds sometimes numbering in the thousands.

Daredevils and extreme stunts have been part of Niagara's official history since the beginning of the 20th century. The most popular stunt, to ride a barrel over Horseshoe Falls, has been repeated multiple times over the years – sometimes successfully, sometimes not.

The first recorded and successful trip was in 1901, by a middle-aged Michigan schoolteacher named Anne Taylor. The barrel was wooden; she was strapped in tightly for the journey, first through the rapids, and then finally plunging over Horseshoe Falls. After completing this stunt, she is quoted as saying,

"No one ought ever do that again." During her time she had achieved a good amount of fame, and she keeps her place today in the history books.

Of course, future daredevils would not heed the advice of Ms. Taylor. In 1911, Bobby Leach successfully toppled over the falls, this time in a steel barrel. It took over six months in a hospital for him to recover from the injuries sustained from the event.

Although the barrel (steel, wooden, or other) has been the most popular device in which to face the Horseshoe Falls, it has not been the only one attempted. A kayak, a jet ski, and even an inner tube have been attempted. Though some survive, many have perished.

Daredevil stunts around Niagara Falls do not occur often. A 1995 attempt was only about the 15th to intentionally survive a trip over the falls since 1901. Moreover, it is illegal to enter the waters of Niagara Falls, both in the United States and Canada. It is part of the Niagara Parks Act. Still, it has not deterred people from risking their lives for a little bit of fame they may never get.

The Niagara River can also be classified as a "strait," since it connects Lake Erie and Lake Ontario.

Area Orientation

Niagara Falls is both a pair of cities and a natural wonder. Foremost, it is the name given to three close but distinct waterfalls along the Niagara River: Horseshoe Falls, Bridal Veil Falls, and American Falls. Two of these falls are in the United States, and most of the third one is in Ontario, Canada. Together, these three Niagara Falls are by far the largest, in terms of volume of water, in North America. Located in the southernmost section of the Golden Horseshoe (Canada's most populous region, which includes the three million plus inhabitants of nearby Toronto), the falls are part of an elaborate natural waterway system connecting all of the Great Lakes. Called the Niagara River, the north-flowing water that feeds Niagara Falls comes almost exclusively from Lake Erie before it makes the trek 35 miles north and dumps into Lake Ontario.

There are actually two cities called "Niagara Falls," and they are across the river from each other. One is in New York State, United States, and the other is in Ontario, Canada. Together, these small cities surround the waterfalls and the various natural phenomena around them. They are connected via two close bridges: the Rainbow Bridge and the Whirlpool Rapids Bridge. Tourists will often hear talk of the "Canadian side of the falls" or "American side of the falls."

Both cities offer views of the landscape and offer their own unique set of attractions and experiences. However, the Canadian side of the falls is much more popular in terms of vista, hotel accommodations, attractions, and overall quality. When people visit Niagara Falls, they are generally talking about Niagara Falls, Ontario, and not Niagara Falls, New York. Still it is common for visitors to cross the international border and visit both sides during their visit.

WHO VISITS NIAGARA FALLS

Niagara Falls has a reputation for being a predominantly wholesome, upbeat vacation destination. It is a very well-established vacation destination that has been attracting a steady stream of visitors for years. In fact, about three quarters of the people visiting the falls are from out of the country; most of them from the United States. As a community, Niagara Falls is surprisingly big. There are about 78,000 people living in Niagara Falls, Ontario, and about 56,000 people living in Niagara Falls, New York.

When people come to Niagara Falls as visitors today, they come for a variety of reasons – whether they are on a family vacation, a singles trip, or on a honeymoon. But at the center of it all, the reason for all the truckloads of people and of the modern attractiveness, is the falls itself.

COUPLES

The "Honeymoon Capital of the World" is known as being a top destination for weddings, honeymoons, and other romantic retreats. Thousands of couples get married around the falls each year, and even more spend quality time there, "away from it all." There are many romantic options for couples, including luxury suites at many of the area hotels, and countless romantic restaurants, some with unparalleled vistas of some of the most famous and romantic waterfalls in the world.

Although Niagara Falls has had a steady stream of tourists since the 1700s, it didn't really achieve commercial success as a romantic hotspot until 1953, when a certain Hollywood movie and a certain Hollywood star put it on the map. That was the year *Niagara,* starring Marilyn Monroe, was released. The movie centers on a love triangle with a young couple honeymooning at the falls.

Though the movie is viewed upon today as rather average (not Monroe's best work), it features many, many shots on location at Niagara Falls. This gave the wide-eyed public a sweeping and romantic view of Niagara, and the tourist industry skyrocketed as a direct result.

It has also been suggested that there is a chemical and biological reason as to why the falls are popular as a romantic spot. The hundreds of thousands of gallons of water falling create negative ions. These ions may help foster a happier mood and fight and even cure diseases.

FAMILIES

In addition to romantic retreats, families of all kinds visit Niagara Falls – it is largely an incredibly family-oriented vacation spot. Even the youngest children will appreciate the majesty of Horseshoe Falls, and the thrill of some of the area's falls-centered attractions. For older children and teens, Clifton Hill offers arcades, wax museums, a few rides, and a nice selection of kid-friendly restaurants.

TOUR GROUPS

The falls are also extremely popular with tour groups coming from nearby cities. Many times, those visiting Toronto,

Hamilton, or Buffalo will take an afternoon expedition to Niagara Falls, without any intent to spend the night. They will arrive, step out onto one of the several available viewing platforms (both on the United States' side and the Canadian side), perhaps get a quick bite to eat, and then head back. It takes about 30 minutes to get to the falls from the Buffalo area, an hour from Hamilton, and maybe two hours from Toronto.

SINGLES

Though singles make frequent trips to the falls, it is less common to visit alone. This is different from places such as Atlantic City, where people will frequently visit by themselves. However, in my opinion, this is an underrated group because there is much to do at Niagara Falls that can be enjoyed by only one person. There are lots of great bars and a few night-clubs. Vacationing in the area for singles frequently centers on the availability of legalized gambling – there are two major casinos in Niagara Falls, Ontario, and one immediately across the border, in New York State. However, Toronto as a vacation destination is far more popular with singles.

THINGS TO DO IN NIAGARA FALLS

At Niagara Falls, there's never a shortage of things to do. In fact, with such a variety of attractions here, visitors can go for days without so much as a glimpse of the waterfalls. There are so many museums, restaurants, resorts, parks, and more in Niagara Falls and the greater Niagara region that you may – if only for a moment – forget where it all began. This book will take you through the varied attractions in Niagara

Falls proper, and point out some of the headliners from the greater Niagara region.

Niagara Falls' prime tourist season runs during the spring, summer, and fall, roughly from Memorial Day to Labor Day. During the peak summer times, the crowds throng the region and the attractions are in full swing. The hottest season, in July, sees average temperatures in the mid-80s (Fahrenheit).

Conversely, during the off season and colder winter months, the average high temperature drops to about 31°F in January. Plus, many of the attractions are closed – particularly the outdoor and falls-related activities (though the falls themselves are always accessible for viewing). A visit during the wintertime can help the budget traveler save a lot of money on hotel stays; and there are still many attractions open during the wintertime. For convenience, this book will denote which attractions are not open year-round by having a "seasonal" flag at the end of the attraction listing.

EXPLORE THE FALLS

These important attractions are the main draw to Niagara Falls. There are many different ways you can see the falls – the surrounding parks, the famous boat rides, the caves, the mist, and peering over the brink. Before you do anything else in Niagara Falls, see Niagara Falls.

VISIT AREA ATTRACTIONS

Historical museums, national landmarks, natural wonders (other than the falls) seem to be everywhere. Tourists can visit historic forts, animal exhibits, skyscraping buildings, theme and amusement parks, and much more.

PLAY ON CLIFTON HILL

Whether you call it tacky or fun, if it is a tourist trap that you seek, look no further than Clifton Hill. If you're in need of a theme restaurant, dark rides, huge video arcades, or more wax museums than you may ever see again, you need to visit this favorite area. Complete with huge signage and the brightness of noon at midnight (and countless throngs of people), Clifton Hill is the most famous attraction area outside of the falls themselves.

SEE THE GREATER NIAGARA REGION

There's much more to Niagara than the falls! A short drive outside of the city proper will bring visitors into the glorious Niagara wine country, filled with history, art, and a truly calm atmosphere. Beautiful small towns and villages, drives through endless miles of vine-land and forest, and that sweet smell of nature with a hint of tourism. After all, six million of the 18 million visitors to the Niagara region do not visit the falls.

GETTING INFORMATION

The more you know about Niagara Falls before you go, the more you can do, and the more fun you'll have. Not only will you better appreciate your time, the anticipation of seeing the sights will be that much greater.

NIAGARA FALLS TOURISM

(5400 Robinson St. ☎ 905.356.6061 🖱 niagarafallstourism.com)
Niagara Falls Tourism is the official Canadian tourism site for the city of Niagara Falls. The site contains extremely thorough

listings of attractions and more in the Niagara Falls area, both for Ontario and New York.

Promotional booklets and fliers containing area information may be available (which are oftentimes full color and beautifully designed) and are funded by the businesses themselves and the Authority. Therefore, information obtained via these sources is biased, but it still offers up enough details to give visitors a thorough idea of the area's offerings.

NIAGARA FALLS, CANADA

(🖱 niagarafalls.ca) This is the official Web site for the City of Niagara Falls on the Canadian side. In addition to providing tourist information, it also provides details on public transportation and other city services. A very comprehensive Web site.

NIAGARA FALLS, NEW YORK

(🖱 niagarafallsusa.org) This is the official Web site for the City of Niagara Falls, New York. It provides tourist information, city services, transportation, and other city-related and governmental information.

NIAGARA-USA

(🖱 niagara-usa.com) On the American side, Niagara-USA provides comprehensive information of the region, not just for Niagara Falls, but also for the greater Niagara USA area.

LUNDY'S LANE TOURIST DISTRICT

(🖱 lundyslane.org) Lundy's Lane is a two-mile stretch of road about three miles west of Niagara Falls, which offers mostly motels and a few attractions. This Web site offers a list of the motels and attractions on Lundy's Lane.

SEASONS AND TEMPERATURES

Niagara Falls' tourism commerce increases exponentially during the summertime. Though there are an increasing number of year-round attractions (casinos, indoor waterparks, and more), the bulk of activity is during the hot summer months.

SPRING

(Average High: 55° F; Average Low: 35° F) Before the tourist season, temperatures get warm and popular summer attractions begin to open. There can be some good bargains in the spring.

SUMMER

(Average High: 82° F; Average Low: 61° F) Summertime is when most tourists visit the falls. The weather can be hot, but all the attractions are open and in full swing. Expect long (sometimes very long!) lines, expensive accommodations, and throngs of people in every corner of town.

FALL

(Average High: 55° F; Average Low: 38° F) After the end of October, the bulk of Niagara's summertime attractions are closed for the season, so prices and tourist numbers start to drop rapidly.

WINTER

(Average High: 31° F; Average Low: 17° F) The chilly, snowy wintertime of Niagara makes for fewer outdoor attractions, cheaper room rates, and some pretty spectacular wintry formations by the falls and Great Gorge. If you want to brave the cold (and don't care about **Maid of the Mist** being closed), you'll save a bundle and see some interesting Niagara Falls sights.

PACKING FOR YOUR TRIP

Knowing where to go is one thing, but you'll need to pack the right equipment to have a good time. Remember, pack what you *think* you'll need. A good suitcase isn't only filled with things you know you'll use, but also what you *might* use. This section provides some tips on packing the right items for your vacation. But don't worry; if you do end up forgetting something, chances are you can buy a cheap one at your destination.

CLOTHES AND TOILETRIES

Of course, pack to reflect your destination and your plans! The lake effect causes intense snow and freezing in the winter, and summertime can be very hot (sometimes 90°F or more), and summertime rain and wintertime snow are common. As a guideline, it's best to pack for at least one additional day. If your trip is three nights, bring four changes of clothes. Keep in mind that many resorts in Niagara Falls have laundry-cleaning capabilities; using them may reduce your overall luggage.

Basic toiletries are cheap and small and widely accessible, so even if you do forget something, in many cases they might be cheap to replace, or even free – many hotels offer free toiletry items (razors, toothbrushes) to guests upon request.

MEDICATIONS AND OTHER ITEMS

Make sure you have all necessary medications with you before leaving home. Keep important medicines close to you at all times. Also, don't forget sunscreen, camera, film and batteries, bathing suit, sunglasses, contact lenses, warm coat, rain jacket, waist pack, purse, long socks, a nice set of clothes (for a nice dinner), packed food for munching, driver's license or photo identification (you may need your passport to cross the border), and whatever else your vacation may call for.

GETTING THERE

Niagara Falls is *not* a major city. It does not have a major airport, though it is close to several. When planning a trip to Niagara Falls, most people from out of state will fly into one of the major area airports, rent a car, and drive to the falls. Others will take public transportation.

ARRIVING BY PLANE

There are three major airports within 90 miles of Niagara Falls. Two of them are in Canada and one is in the United States. Depending on the point of origin, which airport a visitor chooses can affect price, travel time, and hassle (for example, whether or not one has to go through customs).

The closest major metropolitan area to Niagara Falls by far is Buffalo, New York. At about 21 miles away, Buffalo has an international airport called the **Buffalo Niagara International Airport** (airport code: BUF), which has many flights with major carriers. The airport is a part of the Niagara Frontier Transportation Authority. Car rentals are available either on the property or nearby. Additionally, there are shuttle buses that will take visitors directly to Niagara Falls.

The Canadian city of Hamilton has the next closest airport. The city itself is about 45 miles away. The **John C. Munro Hamilton International Airport** (airport code: YHM) serves the area, which has more than 600,000 residents including the surrounding area.

For those interested in visiting the most populous city in Canada, urban metropolis Toronto is about 80 miles away, and the **Lester B. Pearson International Airport** (airport code: YYZ) is only 15 miles away from the city's center. There is much to do in Toronto, and many famous sites that one would expect from a large city of over three million residents. But this book is not about Toronto, so you're going to have to head out of town.

There are numerous transportation services that will take visitors from any of these airports into Niagara Falls. One of these is the **Niagara Air Bus** (🖱 *niagaraairbus.com)*, which will pick up tourists from any of these three airports, and bring them right to their Niagara Falls destination. Additionally, they will accept passengers for transfer between the three airports.

ARRIVING BY TRAIN

Passenger rail service **Amtrak** (🖱 *amtrak.com)* stops in both Niagara Falls, Ontario, and Niagara Falls, New York. Amtrak train routes are limited, but work exceptionally well when coming from the east (Chicago/Detroit) or the West (New York/New England).

Customs however, can greatly increase the wait time when crossing the border by rail, so for those whose final destination is international, it may be much quicker to take the train to the last stop in your departure country, and take a taxi across the border. Both stations are only a few short miles to the border, though the New York station is a bit more desolate.

For those traveling within Canada, the **Via Rail** (🖱 *viarail.com*) system connects most of the major cities in Canada, including as far west as Vancouver all the way to Halifax.

ARRIVING BY BUS

As a national bus service, **Greyhound** makes regular stops in all the surrounding cities, where you may either catch local public transportation or arrange other means to get to the falls.

For those coming from Buffalo, New York, the **Niagara Frontier Transit Authority** provides public transportation (bus and limited rail) to much of the area, including a bus route to Niagara Falls.

Other bus programs and charters are available. Since Niagara Falls is so heavily traveled, many people are always in need of bus or charter services from the local airports, and train and bus stations. When making reservations for your trip, contact the closest reasonable destination where you are in need of transportation (your destination airport or station where you require bus service to the falls). They will have information as to what services are available.

ARRIVING BY CAR

Niagara Falls has a prime Great Lakes region location that allows easy access driving from many major cities. Toronto, New York City, Boston, and even Detroit are well within a day's drive. Driving from Chicago is possible, but it will take up most of your day.

Most visitors arrive at Niagara Falls by driving from the United States; either from driving all the way, or from arriving by plane and renting a car at the airport. In any case, arriving from the United States into the Niagara Falls section of Ontario requires passage over one of three area bridges. They are, from north to south: the Queenston-Lewiston Bridge, the Whirlpool Bridge, and the Rainbow Bridge. A total of four bridges cross the Niagara River (the fourth bridge is upstream and not in the Niagara Falls area). Each of these bridges can be very crowded, as they are all stationed with an army of customs officers, no matter which way you are traveling. The most popular bridge is the Rainbow Bridge, as it is the closest to Niagara Falls and offers the best views.

CROSSING THE BORDER

Niagara Falls is located in between two different countries, and exploring both of them will require knowledge of customs, exchange rates, taxes and such. This section highlights some of this important travel information for those traveling in between the United States and Canada.

CUSTOMS

The two cities of Niagara Falls are exactly on the border, which makes getting back and forth between attractions a bit interesting. Granted, most travelers will stay in Canada for the duration of their stay, but they will be looking at the United States when viewing most of the falls. Plus, the Rainbow Bridge border crossing is almost directly across the street from Clifton Hill.

That being said, border crossing from Canada to the United States is very easy if you are a Canadian or U.S. Citizen and you have a valid passport. On many occasions, they also accept other government-issued I.D.s, but it is usually best to carry your passport when crossing into another country.

Border officials aren't the friendliest folk, but they aren't supposed to be. After all, it is their job to question everything since they are protecting their respective countries, so treat them with respect and *do not* make light of the formalities – they have every right (and responsibility) to check and in some cases, prevent anybody from crossing the border, regardless of citizenship. So be kind and professional, and you should cross the border without difficulty (except for the frequent traffic jam).

If you are crossing the border in some manner other than by car (and sometimes with a car) you will probably be asked to fill out a customs declaration form. This form can be completed prior to your arrival in the destination country, maybe on the plane before landing. It will ask you about any goods or currency you are carrying into the country. Produce, livestock, and large sums of money will be questioned, and in some cases, taxed or even confiscated. You may be required to fill this form out whether or not you are a citizen of the destination country.

EXCHANGE RATE

Canadian currency should be obtained prior to entering Canada, or at an official bank or money exchange location. Most places in Niagara Falls, Ontario, will accept U.S. currency. However, many places will exchange currency at an unfavorable rate. This is *not* a recommended spending habit. Instead, travelers wishing to use credit cards for purchases in Canada tend to receive a more favorable exchange rate from their credit card company.

METRIC CONVERSIONS

Canada uses the metric system; distances are expressed in kilometers (50 miles is about 80 kilometers), and temperatures are expressed in Celsius (20°C is about 68°F). There are specific conversion formulas available all over the Internet, but generally U.S. travelers get accustomed to the system within a few hours of exposure.

TOURIST AREAS

While the American side of the falls is basically a lump of attractions in and around the **Niagara Falls State Park**, the Canadian side has conveniently been divided up into different "tourist sections." Each of these sections both in the U.S. and Canada has hotels, restaurants, and attractions, but each has its own unique flavor:

AMERICAN SIDE OF THE FALLS

With little organization, the American side of the falls contains a chunk of tourist attractions, a casino-hotel, and hotels and motels.

CLIFTON HILL

Clifton Hill is the major tourist section on the Canadian side of the falls. Here is where visitors will find most of the wax museums, amusement attractions, rides, themed restaurants, and a major casino. The few hotels here are small, noisy, and right in the middle of all that tourist-trap wonderment.

FALLSVIEW

Overlooking Horseshoe Falls is the aptly named Fallsview section. Other than a few restaurants and another larger casino, this is the major resort section of town. Here visitors will find all the towering hotels cramped together, each vying for their view of the falls below. For the most romantic and luxurious Niagara Falls vacation, visitors choose to stay in the resorts of Fallsview.

WHIRLPOOL

The smallest of the tourist areas, the Whirlpool section surrounds the Niagara Whirlpool and Rapids. Smaller bed and breakfasts are found in this area, as well as golf courses and a few scattered restaurants.

LUNDY'S LANE

The more inexpensive hotels and motels are located along Lundy's Lane, a few miles west of the falls. Here are more chain restaurants, miniature golf and go-carts, and motor lodges galore. Lundy's Lane features many shopping options (including outlet malls), both for locals and tourists. Lundy's Lane stretches about two miles west to the edge of town.

GETTING AROUND

The major Niagara Falls tourist district is in a fairly compact area surrounding the falls. Clifton Hill, Murray Hill (or "Falls-view"), **Table Rock Point**, and **Maid of the Mist** (the major attractions) are all within walking distance, if you do not object to walking over a mile. There is also plenty of parking all across the area, most of which requires payment either in a meter or in a private lot. However, there are modes of public transportation as well, so vacationing without a car is not only economical, it's likely easier.

NIAGARA TRANSIT

(4320 Bridge St. ☎ 905.356.1179 🖱 niagaratransit.com) The Niagara Transit is the public transportation system for Niagara Falls, and has been since 1960. Though it operates several bus lines around the area, the only ones tourists need to be concerned with are the three Falls Shuttles, which are the Red Line, Green Line, and Blue Line of buses. These bring passengers to the tourism sectors of Niagara Falls, and travel as far north as the Whirlpool Rapids and as far south as the Chippewa Business District.

Niagara Transit buses operate year-round. Cost for the Falls Shuttle service is more expensive than the other lines run by Niagara Transit, but they offer ride-all-day prices. For more specific information and map routes, visit their Web site. *($)*

PEOPLE MOVER

(🖱 niagaraparks.com) Niagara Parks manages an additional mode of transportation: the People Mover System. These buses mainly transport tourists to the various attractions owned by the Niagara Parks system. However, these buses only operate seasonally (with no service during the colder months). People Mover access prices are per day, and offer unlimited use. The hours are not very generous and they change very frequently, so check ahead on their Web site for the most up-to-date information. *($)*

NIAGARA SCENIC TROLLEY

(Within the Niagara Falls State Park) One of the easiest ways to take in all of the United States' side of the falls is on the **Niagara Scenic Trolley**. With regular year-round routes throughout the **Niagara Falls State Park**, the trolley makes several stops at several key points throughout the park, including the Visitors Center. The trolley covers about three miles on its journey. *($)*

FALLS INCLINE RAILWAY

(☗ niagaraparks.com) The most memorable legitimate transportation offering is also managed by Niagara Parks – the Falls Incline Railway. For those staying in the Fallsview section of town, the Horseshoe Falls and **Table Rock Point** are much closer than the Clifton Hill Section. So, to navigate the steep incline between the Fallsview section and Horseshoe Falls is an incline railway, which brings visitors up and down the short hill. Like the People Mover System, this mode of transport is only open in warmer months, so wintertime visitors will have to walk (or drive) to the falls. *($)*

NIAGARA FRONTIER TRANSIT AUTHORITY

(☗ nfta.com) While certainly not dedicated to tourists, the New York side of the falls offers a network of public transportation bus service through the Buffalo Niagara region. Primarily dedicated to commuters, these buses (and limited commuter rail) can get you all around the Niagara Falls region, the Buffalo airport, and area attractions on the New York side of the falls. Check their Web site for specific routes, times, and pricing information. *($)*

TAXI SERVICES

Taxis are available on both the American and Canadian sides of the falls, and at most of the major hotels and attractions. They are available for transportation locally around town. Taxis may take passengers across the border for additional costs. For more information, contact your hotel.

BRIDGES

Although there have been as many as 12 bridges crossing the Niagara River, today that number is vastly reduced. Now there are a total of four auto/commuter bridges that cross the Niagara River along its 35-mile stretch from Lake Erie to Lake Ontario. Three of these bridges, operated by the **Niagara Falls Bridge Commission** (🖱 *niagarafallsbridges.com*), are within the vicinity of Niagara Falls. The commission is a partnership between the United States and Canada. Each bridge crossing is a step into a foreign country, and thus each trek across them will require a passage through customs. These bridges also require separate tolls.

QUEENSTON-LEWISTON BRIDGE

Furthest north on the Niagara River, this bridge is located just south of the American town of Lewiston and the Canadian town of Queenston. It opened in 1963 and is the same type of bridge as the more famous Rainbow Bridge – though a bit higher over the river.

WHIRLPOOL RAPIDS BRIDGE

South of the whirlpool and rapids, this bridge contains two sections; one for cars and auto traffic, and one for rail traffic.

If you are traveling across the border on Amtrak (or Via Rail) then this is the bridge you will use. The bridge is one of the oldest still in operation, having opened in 1848.

RAINBOW BRIDGE

The most famous bridge crossing the Niagara River also has the best view – it is just a few hundred feet downstream of Horseshoe Falls. Pedestrians frequently cross the bridge on a separate dedicated walkway, which offers great views of evening fireworks and the falls' illumination. This bridge is also the most crowded – expect wait times to be excessive during peak travel times. The Rainbow Bridge opened in 1941.

PEACE BRIDGE

The Peace Bridge opened in 1927 and is the only auto/ commuter bridge across the Niagara River that is not operated by the Niagara Falls Bridge Commission. It is the closest bridge to downtown Buffalo, New York.

Exploring the Falls

⭐

First things first. You've come to Niagara Falls. So before you hang out in Clifton Hill, before you traverse the casinos, before you do *anything*, see the falls. Whether it is on a boat or over the side of the Great Gorge, seeing these falls up close and personal will completely affect how you perceive this wonderful vacation destination.

This section focuses on the major natural attractions within Niagara Falls: the falls themselves, the Whirlpool Rapids, and the surrounding parks and gardens. These are the headlining attractions, and the main draw for millions of people throughout the year.

HORSESHOE FALLS

The Canadian Horseshoe Falls is the most famous waterfall in Niagara Falls, and the most voluminous (and powerful) waterfall in North America. Over 90 percent of the water of the Niagara River flows over Horseshoe Falls (the rest goes over the nearby American Falls and Bridal Veil Falls). Named "Horseshoe" because of its U shape, Horseshoe Falls is also known for creating large amounts of mist, which has become something of a trademark. The mist rises from the center of the U, which occasionally makes Horseshoe Falls difficult to view. Given the right weather conditions, the mist can be visible for miles around.

Since most water from the Great Lakes feeds into the Niagara River, most water from the Great Lakes passes over (or will eventually pass over) Horseshoe Falls. The volume of water going over the falls can be controlled; it fluctuates based on the intake from the area's power plants. Human intervention has reduced the amount of water going over the falls in recent years to as little as 150,000 gallons, but it has been known to handle over 600,000 gallons per second.

The water's maximum freefall from the top of Horseshoe Falls to the river below is an unimpressive 170 feet. Moreover, there are piles of rocks that reduce this freefall for most of the water to as little as 70 feet. However, this waterfall is not famous for height. The Canadian Horseshoe Falls is one of the most extraordinary natural occurrences to behold.

BRIDAL VEIL FALLS

With a span of only 56 feet, the smallest of the three Niagara Falls is Bridal Veil Falls. Named because of its similar appearance to a wedding bride's veil, it is situated immediately next to the American Falls. In fact, it is so close to American Falls, and so similar in appearance, that at first glance it looks like it is part of American Falls. However, there is in fact a small landmass called Luna Island that separates the two of them. Bridal Veil Falls shares many of the same attributes of American Falls, including the cluttered rocks at the bottom that greatly reduce the free fall of the water.

AMERICAN FALLS

The American Falls is the United States' major claim to waterfall fame in the Niagara region. This big, dominant next-door neighbor is hardly as impressive as Horseshoe Falls, but it holds its own in some respects. The total length of the American Falls is 830 feet. However, only about ten percent of the water from the Niagara River goes over the American Falls – most goes over the nearby Horseshoe Falls. This makes the water of the American Falls much easier to control in terms of altering (or even completely stopping) the flow of water.

In fact, for several months in 1969, the flow over American Falls was completely stopped while there was consideration for removal of some rocks. The falls have not been completely stopped since, though in an emergency authorities claim it is possible.

FIREWORKS AND ILLUMINATION

Though daytime is the most popular time to view the falls, there are two nighttime viewing opportunities that have proved very popular: the **Fireworks** and the **Illumination**.

On certain evenings during the busy seasons, later at night (after dusk) and weather permitting, visitors all across the Niagara Falls area will see a glorious fireworks display right over Horseshoe Falls. The display is short but sweet, and offers a nice end to the day. Additionally, the fireworks can be seen during major Canadian and American holidays.

Also, at night, bright beams of colored light illuminate the falls, making them nicely visible when the nighttime and mist would make the falls difficult to see. The falls are lit year-round, but the lighting schedule varies depending on the season.

The falls have been illuminated in some form for many years. The first electrical light-assisted illumination occurred in 1879. It has since then become a staple at Niagara Falls, and a popular thing to see.

For information about specific fireworks and illumination schedules, contact your hotel.

Exploring the Falls

THE GREAT GORGE

Upstream of Niagara Falls, the Niagara River is fairly level with the surrounding land. However, the falls drop the Niagara River 170 feet down. As such, the falls have been cutting through the land over thousands of years, creating a canyon-type geological formation downstream. This section of the river (up to about seven miles from the falls) is called the Great Gorge.

This gorge is the direct result of Niagara Falls' erosion over thousands of years. As the falls progress towards Lake Ontario, they continue to cut through the land, making the gorge longer and longer. The gorge has been forming since the beginnings of Niagara Falls. Following the path of the gorge through its seven-mile stretch can reveal the history and timeline of the falls.

Visitors from the United States may first encounter the gorge when they enter Canada on either the Whirlpool Rapids Bridge or the Rainbow Bridge – both of which cross the gorge. The Great Gorge largely separates the United States and Canada – looking across it presents vistas of the other country.

WHIRLPOOL AND RAPIDS

When the Niagara River struck an underground current a few thousand years ago, it created an aquatic explosion that altered the direction of the Niagara River and created two unique features of the river that are still evident today. These features, the Whirlpool and Rapids, are located two-three miles downstream (north) of the falls. Several attractions allow visitors to explore this section of the river.

Starting at about two miles downstream of Niagara Falls (within the Great Gorge), the river becomes steeper, resulting in some pretty wild and dangerous rapids that continue for about a mile. At this point, the river is a narrow 200 feet across, and it descends about 50 feet in elevation in slightly more than a mile. These factors, along with the 600,000 gallons (at full blast) of water flowing every second, account for the high speed of the water here – about 22 miles per hour. The rapids culminate at the whirlpool, a massive churning, swirling, and dangerous mass of water about 35 feet deep. In fact, the whirlpool and rapids are considered by some to be the most dangerous rapids in the world.

The whirlpool and rapids (collectively called the "Whirlpool Rapids") have been a popular sight since Tourism in Niagara Falls began. One of the first was in the late 1800s, when an incline railway made of wood brought visitors down the gorge and onto a landing where they could view the falls up close. This railway became something of a favorite spot until it was burned down in 1934. Later, a walkway replaced the railway, and it became largely the attraction it is today.

As with the falls, the rapids and whirlpool separate the United States and Canada. On the U.S. side, the **Whirlpool State Park** allows visitors to walk down a pathway towards the rapids. On the Canadian side, the Niagara Parks Commission has several attractions with which one may view the river.

THE FALLS FROM CANADA

The dominant Canadian agency controlling much of the property and attractions related to Niagara Falls on the Canadian side is the Niagara Parks Commission. The **Niagara Parks** (🖰 *niagaraparks.com*) are both a series of attractions and a management company. In a way, it is the National Park Service for Canada's Niagara region. For travelers admiring the falls themselves, or other natural or ecological place of interest within the Niagara Falls area, chances are high that they are on a Niagara Parks property.

The government of Ontario initially created Niagara Parks as the organization to maintain the immediate vicinity around Horseshoe Falls. When established in 1885, the agency managed and operated about 150 acres. Today it manages over 4,000 acres of land and much of the stretch of road alongside the Niagara River. In other words, Niagara Parks is the official Provincial-appointed organization responsible for this natural wonder. It is a complete system within a system, again similar to the NPS, with transportation, a police force, and the like.

Tip: The Commission offers an **Adventure Pass**, which includes admission to the most popular attractions for a discounted price, plus use of the Niagara Parks People Mover. The **Winter Magic Pass** is available in the off season, since there are fewer attractions available in the winter.

MAID OF THE MIST ✪ Must See!

(5920 Niagara Parkway ☎ 905.358.0311 🖰 maidofthemist.com Boarding available from both the U.S. and Canada.) With little doubt, the most famous, most popular, and best attraction in all of Niagara Falls is the Maid of the Mist. This is the quintessential must-see itinerary bullet point. If you do nothing else during your stay in Niagara Falls, you *must* take one of these historic rides.

What is Maid of the Mist? It is a boat ride into the mouth of Niagara Falls. Prior to the 30-minute experience, passengers are provided with raincoats as they board the boat. From there, they are taken to the American Falls, as close as the captain can feasibly navigate. Travelers may experience some splashes and mist from the falls. After a few moments of glorious gawking, the boat steers its way into the mouth of Horseshoe Falls… it is here where the magic takes place.

The boat slowly makes its way into the center of Horseshoe Falls. Enveloped in the mist, surrounded by thousands of gallons of falling water, the boat and all its passengers get positively soaked. This experience is utterly unique and available nowhere else in the world. *This* is why you visit Niagara Falls.

With beginnings dating back as early as the 1840s, the Maid of the Mist is one of America's oldest tourist attractions. However, it began as a transportation company, bringing people and cargo across the Niagara River. Ferry transportation was popular at the time, and boats ranging in size had been operating regular ferry schedules since the early 1930s.

After the first bridge was built over the Niagara River, the need for ferry service was drastically reduced. So instead of merely going between points, they began to operate as a tourist attraction, bringing sightseers up close to the falls. Other than a few interruptions in service, and various fleet changes, the Maid of the Mist has been operating in this capacity, and continues to do so today.

Note: Maid of the Mist is accessible in the U.S. and Canada, both sides providing virtually the same boating experience. The U.S. dock (near the **Observation Tower** in the Niagara Falls

State Park) is less crowded. Also, Maid of the Mist is a seasonal attraction – boats must be out of the water before the Great Gorge's water level drops for the winter. *($$)*

TABLE ROCK POINT ✪ Must See!

If you just can't wait to see the falls, the easiest and quickest way to get that awe-inspiring look at Horseshoe Falls is on the overlook at Table Rock Point. While serving as a main gateway for the Niagara Parks attractions, this section of developed land has the standard tourist amenities, such as a cafeteria and several gift shops. For those using the Niagara Parks tourist shuttles, this area is one of the main transit depots.

This prime location is situated right next to Horseshoe Falls. When visitors step out onto the back patio, they are literally only a few feet from where the water rolls off of the cliff and into the river below. The mist blows in their faces, the water rumbles loudly. This is as close as you can get to this natural wonder – closer even (though considerably drier) than **Maid of the Mist**. The difference being that here, at Table Rock Point, visitors see the top of the falls. Maid takes you to the bottom.

HORSESHOE RAPIDS

Traveling at about 25 miles per hour before toppling over the brink, the rapids above Niagara Falls (and particularly Horseshoe Rapids) stretch far upstream. They can be viewed throughout both the Canadian and American sides, and a walking path on the Canadian side follows the river for great views. It is here in these rapids, where the old scow has been stranded since 1918.

JOURNEY BEHIND THE FALLS ✪ Must See!

(6650 Niagara River Pkwy. ☎ 905.354.1551

🖰 **niagaraparks.com)** The Niagara Parks Commission has made it possible for visitors to admire the falls from many different angles – from above, from below, and in this case, from behind. The Journey Behind the Falls is a year-round attraction that takes visitors down into a narrow shaft and gives them the opportunity to view the back of Horseshoe Falls.

Located at the **Table Rock Point Complex,** visitors are taken in an elevator, down deep into the rock of the Niagara River. When they emerge from their downward trek, they are presented with a long, dimly lit hallway, with cold wet cement surrounding them. There is a faint rumbling. As they walk down the hallway, the noise increases, until they turn left, and see the water – thousands of gallons of it – spilling just a few feet in front of them.

The portal in which visitors can view the falls is small, but sufficient in giving the impression. In warmer weather, visitors may be able to walk out onto a plank that allows a nice view of Horseshoe Falls from mid-way down the gorge. In the wintertime, there is much ice, and the passage is *freezing* cold, so wear multiple layers. *($)*

NIAGARA'S FURY: THE CREATION OF THE FALLS

(At Table Rock, Second Floor) Niagara's Fury: The Creation of the Falls is a theme park-style attraction where visitors are introduced to the geologic history of Niagara Falls by experiencing it via a simulation. After a cute cartoon pre-show, visitors are given raincoats as they enter a circular room and position themselves near the middle. As they stand, the floor trembles, water spills on them (small amounts only), and the 360-degree screen above them depicts several key times of Niagara's formation – including the melting of the glaciers and the exploding of the whirlpool. The raincoats are important, but the water dripping from overhead is unnecessary. Overall, this is a cute attraction, if a bit overpriced. *($$)*

WHIRLPOOL AERO CAR

(3850 Niagara River Pkwy. ☎ 905.354.5711

🖱 **niagaraparks.com)** In addition to the awe-inspiring waterfalls just three miles upstream, the Whirlpool Rapids are the other major natural phenomenon located along this short stretch of the river. The rapids, created by the Niagara Falls' passage through this portion of the river, are a bubbly brew of angry water tossing in many directions. This is where the Niagara River makes a sudden and violent shift in direction. Today, visitors can explore these rapids in a way that the falls themselves cannot be seen – by dangling right above them.

The Whirlpool Aero Car (sometimes called the Spanish Aero Car) allows visitors to get a literal bird's-eye view of the churning rapids from hundreds of feet above. Sort of like a gondola or horizontal ski lift, the aero car is suspended by cables, which are attached to both sides of the Great Gorge. As many as 35-40 visitors board the standing-room-only car, which takes them over the gorge and dangles them for a few moments over the rapids. The total trip is a little more than half a mile.

The aero car is one of the oldest operating man-made attractions in the falls area. Designed by a Spanish engineer, it first opened in 1916. Six strong cables suspend the car and the entire trip takes about ten minutes.

The aero car is open only when the weather permits (it may close during periods of rain, snow, or heavy winds). (Seasonal) *($)*

WHITE WATER WALK

(4330 Niagara Pkwy. 🖱 niagaraparks.com) Just upstream of the Whirlpool Rapids is the White Water Boardwalk, where visitors can stroll near the churning water that precedes the whirlpool. These rapids are among the most powerful in the country. The actual "walk" is short – only a thousand or so feet along a stretch of boardwalk by the rapids, but the attraction takes visitors much closer to the rapids than a standard hard-to-get view from atop the Great Gorge. Visitors are first taken down into the gorge via elevator, where there is a walkway with several viewing spaces to get a more "up close" view of the rapids.

The rapids here are amazing. Rated a category 6, the world's "most difficult," it is rare to see such a roaring mass of water hurtle right past you. At some places along the walk, visitors get close enough to actually feel the splashes of these monstrous waves.

The White Water Walk is likely a descendent of the original "Great Gorge Adventure" which started as early as the late 1800s, when an incline railway brought tourists down to near the bottom of the gorge. A fire destroyed the railway in the 1930s, and after several rebirths, the walkway of today eventually made its way onto the scene. (Seasonal) *($)*

WHIRLPOOL JET BOAT TOURS

(61 Melville St. ☎ 905.468.4800 🖱 whirlpooljet.com) Located a few miles downstream, in the city of Niagara-on-the-Lake, is the Whirlpool Jet Boat Tours. This positively thrilling boat ride takes visitors speeding at up to 65 miles per hour through the whirlpool and rapids on an 18-mile journey up and down the Niagara River. These boats are designed especially to handle the Niagara Rapids – some of the world's most dangerous rapids. Visitors have the option of taking the "Wet Jet" (where they get absolutely soaked; bring a change of clothes) or the "Dome Jet" (where they are protected from the water by a dome). The entire ride lasts about an hour. The attraction is seasonal, open only during the warmer months of the year. (Seasonal) *($$$$)*

CANADIAN PARKS AND GARDENS

In addition to the falls-based activities, the Niagara Parks Commission operates and manages many of the area's parks and gardens. Some of these parks offer views of Niagara Falls, whereas others are peaceful and reclusive sanctuaries. Still others serve as the habitat for incredible animal and plant life. Many of these parks are located on the Niagara River Parkway, which follows the Niagara River on the Canadian side. Camping, picnicking, fishing, and other such outdoor activities may require permits issued by the Niagara Parks Commission. Contact them prior to arranging your visit if you plan to do anything that may require a permit.

Along the Canadian side of the falls are many picnic areas that may have tables, fire pits, or barbeques. Among these are **Kings Bridge Park**, **Niagara Glen**, and **McFarland Park**. As the facilities and rules for picnic areas differ (such as whether pets are allowed, or whether parking is available), visitors should check the information online beforehand (🖰 *niagaraparks.com*).

QUEEN VICTORIA PARK

(Next to Horseshoe Falls ☻ niagaraparks.com) One of the first parks operated by the Niagara Parks Commission, Queen Victoria Park is truly one of the best "natural" environments in Niagara Falls. The park is largely a nicely decorated and maintained garden, with various seasonal flowers and plants. It features nice walkways and, most importantly, it is very close to Horseshoe Falls (a walkable distance). Many consider it to be the "main" park of the Niagara Parks commission. It is open year-round, with free admission and a regular rotation of international and domestic herpetological displays and a rock garden. It is a romantic, albeit frequently busy, park.

FLORAL CLOCK

(14004 Niagara River Pkwy. ☻ niagaraparks.com) The floral clock is an odd attraction location just outside of the Niagara Falls area. A real clock it is – made almost entirely of floral arrangements that change several times a year. Complete with a large hour, minute, and second hand, the large clock chimes on a regular basis. The face of the clock lies on a plane on the ground, easily viewed from the walking path nearby. It is open to the public during the warmer months.

QUEENSTON HEIGHTS PARK

(14184 Niagara Pkwy. ☻ niagaraparks.com) A few miles north on the Niagara Parkway from the falls brings visitors to the Queenston Heights Park. It was on this site in 1812 where Major General Isaac Brock, a leader for the British during the War of 1812, was killed in action. The Battle of Queenston Heights is often considered Canada's most important battle fought on home soil. Though it is argued that the War of 1812 had no winner, at Queenston Heights the Americans surrendered and the British were victorious. There is a tall monument on this site dedicated to Major General Brock, visible for several miles around.

NAVY ISLAND

(● niagaraparks.com) Visitors may only access this small spot of land about three miles upriver of Horseshoe Falls by boat. There are no facilities on the island, but travel is heavily regulated there. Travelers may opt to camp overnight on the island, hike, or enjoy nature, but only with the permission of the Niagara Parks Commission. Named by the French in the 1700s (as they used to build ships there), the island has a complex history as being private, public, and the location of a hotel at one point. But today, it is being kept undisturbed, and visitors are expected to help maintain its integrity.

DUFFERIN ISLANDS

(● niagaraparks.com) Located just upstream of Horseshoe Falls, Dufferin Islands is a ten-acre nature sanctuary. There are strolling paths and picnic grounds. Additionally, the park has recently become a popular fishing spot for tourists. You can't take your catch home from here though – the "catch and release" program requires all fish to be returned to whence they came. For permit information, call ☎ *800.387.7011.*

NIAGARA GLEN

(● niagaraparks.com) Near the Whirlpool Rapids area, the Niagara Glen is a series of walking or hiking paths that include trails in and around the Great Gorge. These two-plus miles of trails are not always easy, and there is always a regular supply of animal life on hand. This park is open all year, but sometimes may close because of inclement weather.

KINGS BRIDGE PARK

(● niagaraparks.com) Located upstream of the falls, Kings Bridge Park serves mostly families and picnickers. The park boasts a play area for children. Limited facilities, such as washrooms are available.

OAKES GARDEN THEATRE

(● niagaraparks.com) Adjacent to **Queen Victoria Park**, the Oakes Garden Theatre is a small amphitheater suitable for various forms of outdoor entertainment, such as concerts and wedding ceremonies. It is an intimate, natural setting. Contact the Niagara Parks Commission for information on performance schedules.

NIAGARA PARKS GREENHOUSE

(**7145 Niagara Pkwy.** ● niagaraparks.com) The Niagara Parks Greenhouse is a year-round greenhouse attraction that showcases a regular rotation of horticulture throughout the year. At over 10,000 square feet, the greenhouse features both indoor and outdoor exhibits, several exotic birds and butterflies, and even a special garden for the visually impaired.

BOTANICAL GARDENS

(**2565 Niagara Pkwy.** ● niagaraparks.com) Visitors to the Botanical Gardens will enjoy several themed gardens with rotating plant life throughout the year. A major presence at the gardens is the **School of Horticulture**, where students get hands-on botanical experience along with traditional classroom education. The garden was originally a school when it was established in 1936, but in 1990 it became an official botanical garden. The **Butterfly Conservatory** is located on the Botanical Gardens property.

NIAGARA PARKS RECREATION TRAIL

(🖱 niagaraparks.com) The Niagara River extends from Lake Erie to Lake Ontario, separating two countries and in effect creating a peninsula on both the Canadian and American sides. On the Canadian side of the river, the Niagara Parks Recreation Trail is a walking and biking path that follows nearly the entire length of the Niagara River. From **Fort George** in the north to **Fort Erie** in the south, the trail follows the 35-mile length of the river. The trail is almost entirely breakless, so those with a strong athletic sense (and perhaps practicing for a marathon) can enjoy the stretch almost entirely without interruption – not to mention passing through some beautiful landscape. Note: although open year-round, the trail is not managed in the wintertime, so there is frequent snow.

THE FALLS FROM THE AMERICAN SIDE

In the United States, one would be hard-pressed to differentiate Niagara Falls, New York from any other small upstate town. Aside from a small collection of hotels and attractions around the falls, and the towering **Seneca Niagara Casino**, the American side of the falls has little to distinguish itself as one of the most-visited vacation destinations in the country. It is only when visitors approach almost the brink of the falls themselves where they see that the American side has a few attractions as well.

Tip: If you plan on visiting multiple paid attractions within the State Park, consider taking advantage of the **Discovery Pass**, which is a pay-one-price pass that allows admission for multiple attractions at a discount. There are different passes for the winter and summer season, since some attractions are seasonal.

NIAGARA FALLS STATE PARK ✪ Must See!

(☎ 716.278.1976 📱 niagarafallsstatepark.com) Surrounding the immediate Niagara Falls vicinity on the New York side is the Niagara Falls State Park (sometimes called "New York State Park" or "Niagara Reservation State Park"). Started in 1885, the park is the oldest state park in the United States. It was landscape architect Frederick Law Olmsted who was one of the initiators and designers of the Niagara Falls State Park. He is also known for another creation: New York City's Central Park.

The Niagara Falls State Park manages and operates many of the attractions on this side of the falls. The park encompasses all of the American Falls, Bridal Veil Falls, Goat Island (and surrounding islands), and about one third of Horseshoe Falls. Although the park itself is open year-round, including the **Visitors Center**, most of the attractions are seasonal, and thus off-season adventures offer less direct activity with the falls.

The Visitors Center features general information about the falls, including a snack bar and gift shop. The large garden outside is maintained seasonally. Also in the Visitors Center is the **Festival Theater**, a year-round attraction which features the 1999 History Channel movie, *Niagara Falls: A History of the Falls.*

While most Niagara Falls visitors will agree that the Canadian side of the falls is superior, with better views of all that great water, a distinct advantage to the American side is much closer access to the falls themselves, by actually standing "on top" of them (plus, visitors get a great view of Canada).

While in the State Park, visitors without a car may take advantage of the **Niagara Scenic Trolley**, which makes stops at the most popular places within the park.

MAID OF THE MIST ✪ Must See!

(In Niagara Falls State Park ☎ 716.284.8897

⬤ **maidofthemist.com Boarding available from both the U.S. and Canada.)** Maid of the Mist has a loading dock on the American side of the falls, which offers a near-identical experience to its more popular (and more crowded) Canadian counterpart. Regardless of which side of the falls you climb on board these historic boats, it is still a must-see experience, and the best attraction in Niagara Falls. For more information, see "The Falls from Canada" section.

GOAT ISLAND

(In the Niagara Falls State Park) Goat Island is the piece of land that separates Bridal Veil Falls from Horseshoe Falls. Accessible by car and part of the **Niagara Falls State Park**, Goat Island has an interesting location. From here, visitors can see the rapids up close, which lead to the American/Bridal Veil Falls and Horseshoe Falls. It is additionally the location of several of the park's best attractions. Though the island is big, because of its location and the surrounding hostile waters, it is slowly eroding and will disappear as the three Niagara Falls move upstream over many years.

Goat Island is where several of the Niagara Falls State Park attractions are located, including **Cave of the Winds**. Shuttles take visitors around Goat Island and throughout the park, but there are additionally many walking paths on which to stroll endlessly, and benches to sit on and contemplate the scenic vistas.

Given the island's status as a state park, it is largely outdoors, with plenty of wooded paths and river/falls vistas along the way.

LUNA ISLAND

(In the Niagara Falls State Park) Luna Island is the tiny island that separates the Bridal Veil Falls from the American Falls. It is accessible on foot, but no cars are allowed (the island is so small, more than a few cars wouldn't fit anyway). The walkway to Luna Island is on Goat Island. The walk to Luna Island is worth it, as it situates you in between two waterfalls, which is an unusual place to be.

AMERICAN RAPIDS

(In the Niagara Falls State Park) The rapids approaching the American Falls – visible only on the American side, roar through the middle of the park and around the several small islands before toppling over the brink of the American Falls. The rapids reach speeds of up to 25 miles per hour. At night, they may be illuminated with bright spotlights for a more unusual view.

TERRAPIN POINT

(In the Niagara Falls State Park) Horseshoe Falls is bordered on the Canadian side by **Table Rock Point** and on the

American side by Terrapin Point. Here, visitors can feel the mist of Horseshoe Falls as they look across the gorge at Canada. More remote than Table Rock Point, Terrapin Point has great views of the **Canadian Fallsview** resort sections, and the mist here can be just as powerful as Table Rock, if the conditions are right.

CAVE OF THE WINDS ✪ Must See!

(On Goat Island ☎ 716.278.1730) The curious name of this quintessential attraction is misleading. Cave of the Winds is not a cave, but rather a walkway that leads visitors over to the base of Bridal Veil Falls – the smallest of the three Niagara Falls.

Cave of the Winds, however, *used* to be a cave. Named after Aeolus, the Greek God of Wind, it stood behind Bridal Veil Falls and was a popular tourist spot as early as the 1800s. The earliest tourists had to climb down a rope – and eventually a staircase – to reach the cave. However, there were occasionally cave-ins, which killed or injured tourists. It was intentionally destroyed in 1955 because it was in danger of collapsing.

Visitors are given a poncho and special footwear prior to commencing the hour-long adventure. In groups, they are led with a tour guide down an elevator to near the base of Bridal Veil Falls. From there, they walk on a wooden walkway to what has been dubbed the "Hurricane Deck" – the closest accessible point to the falls. It is at this point where visitors get positively *soaked*, sometimes even more than on **Maid of the Mist**. Ice makes the attraction largely inaccessible in the winter, and also requires the decks to be completely re-built each year – a process which can take weeks. (Seasonal) *($)*

OBSERVATION TOWER

(Niagara Falls State Park ☎ 716.278.1796) Located just beyond the Visitors Center in the **Niagara Falls State Park**, the Observation Tower·is the best place in the United States to view the American and Horseshoe Falls. The tower extends out a little bit from the mainland, but still does not come close to the spectacular views from the Canadian side of the falls. Still, the tower offers a very different point of view than the one most visitors are used to. Also, there is a **Maid of the Mist** dock at the Observation Tower. When boarding here, the tour encompasses basically the same experience. However, near the dock, there is (when weather permits) a path where visitors can walk up next to the American Falls – kind of like the **Cave of the Winds**, but you don't get as wet. *($)*

WHIRLPOOL STATE PARK

(Whirlpool Rapids Area ☎ 716.284.4691) Located on the American side of the Whirlpool Rapids area, the Whirlpool State Park is a hearty adventurer's place. Here, a crude cement staircase makes a long descent into the Great Gorge, down nearly to the water level of the rapids. For those who don't wish to make the difficult descent, there is still the perfect place for picnics and play on the upper level, with great views of the whirlpool and rapids. *($)*

THE FALLS FROM THE AIR

You can see Niagara Falls from a bridge, from up close, from a tall building, from inside, and even from behind, but until you see them from high up in the air, you haven't gotten the full falls perspective. It is such an unusual and fantastic way to see the falls, that it's not uncommon for people to exchange marriage vows high above them! Call them in advance for hours and rates.

These attractions are located on both sides of the border. A 🇺🇸 denotes an American-side attraction, and a 🇨🇦 denotes a Canadian-side attraction.

RAINBOW AIR HELICOPTERS

(🇺🇸 454 Main St. ☎ 716.284.2800) Get great views of Niagara Falls and the surrounding countryside on a short flight, which circles the Niagara Falls area. This helicopter tour establishment is very close to the Rainbow Bridge and the falls, so the "getting there" flight time to the falls is much shorter – the ride time is almost cut in half from other helicopter tours, which are located as far as several miles north of the falls. *($$$$)*

NIAGARA HELICOPTERS

(🇨🇦 3731 Victoria Ave. ☎ 905.357.5672 niagarahelicopters.com) The Niagara Helicopters offers tours of the Niagara River and Niagara Falls on a pre-determined tourist route; the entire experience lasts about 12 minutes. On the route, see many of the famous area landmarks, culminating in the famous falls themselves. Charter and photography excursions may also be available. *($$$$)*

NATIONAL HELICOPTERS

(🇨🇦 Niagara District Airport ☎ 905.641.2222 nationalhelicopters.com) National Helicopters whizzes visitors around in a helicopter for a splendid aerial view of several landmark attractions. Aerial tours are available to see Niagara Falls as well as parts of the surrounding wine country. Different packages and tours are available. Also available are charter tours and tours for photography. *($$$$)*

NIAGARA POWER PRODUCTION

There have been hydroelectric plants harnessing the energy of the river for as long as the technology has been available. In fact, one of the first (if not *the* first) hydroelectric alternating current (AC) power plant was installed at Niagara. Today, there are several operating hydroelectric plants on the Niagara River near the falls – both on the American and Canadian sides. These plants provide power to much of the surrounding area. Water is diverted from the river (thus reducing the flow of Niagara Falls) on a regular and tightly controlled basis. The Niagara Power Project manages this camaraderie between the two nations. The water intake center is located a few hundred feet upstream of Niagara Falls, in Ontario, and the water is diverted underground to its destinations several miles downstream.

These attractions are located on both sides of the border. A ▆ denotes an American-side attraction, and a 🍁 denotes a Canadian-side attraction.

ROBERT MOSES NIAGARA POWER PLANT
(▆ **5777 Lewiston Rd. ☎ 716.285.3211**) On the American side, the New York Power Authority (🖱 *nypa.gov*) operates the Robert Moses Niagara Power Plant and Lewiston pump-generating plant. Tours of the on-site **Power Vista** center gives people an overview of how hydroelectric power works,

and how the Robert Moses/Lewiston plants operate. The plant itself is located about 4.5 miles downstream, in Lewiston (north of Niagara Falls). *($)*

SIR ADAM BECK GENERATING STATION
(🍁 Near Queenston Bridge ☎ 905.357.2379) Along the Canadian side of the river are several power generating stations, all named for Sir Adam Beck, an electricity advocate. The Sir Adam Beck Generating Station No. 2, located near Queenston, offers guided tours, vistas, and educational facilities as part of the Niagara Parks Commission. *($)*

Created in 1909, The "International Boundary Waters Treaty" was the first official agreement between the United States and Canada about how to manage power production along the Niagara River.

Horseshoe Falls and the Maid of the Mist

Journey behind the Falls

Horseshoe Falls, Bridal Veil Falls, American Falls, and the Great Gorge

The Rainbow Bridge

Skylon Tower

Mist rises from Horseshoe Falls

Maid of the Mist passing American Falls

The Falls from the air

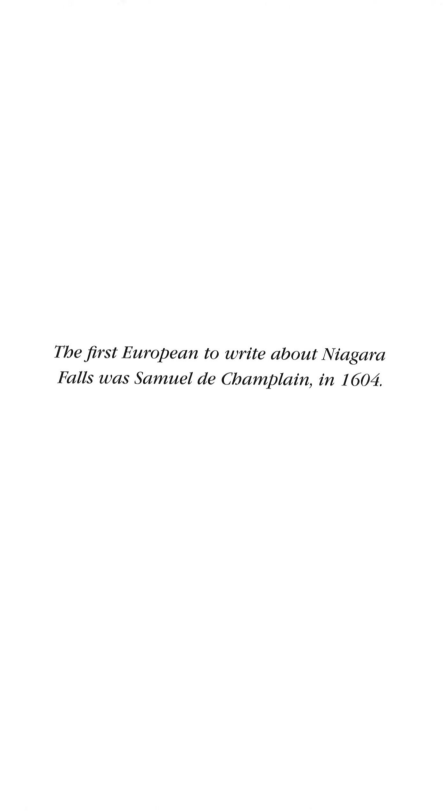

The first European to write about Niagara Falls was Samuel de Champlain, in 1604.

Area Attractions

Niagara Falls is filled with such diverse and unique attractions that it is impossible to categorize them. This section has divided up these attractions (as closely as possible) by type. Some are on the Canadian side, others are on the American side (use the flags to differentiate). This is where the fun continues; when you've explored the falls and you still want more to do, these attractions can keep you busy for weeks. Be prepared for extreme diversity; this section really does run the gamut of possibilities.

These attractions are located on both sides of the border. A ▤ denotes an American-side attraction, and a ◼ denotes a Canadian-side attraction.

OBSERVATION TOWERS

You can get a great view from pretty much any falls-facing area on the Canadian side. This includes hotel rooms, viewing platforms, restaurants, and – of course – observation decks. The higher the point, in general, the better the available view.

SKYLON TOWER ✪ Must See!

(◼ 5200 Robinson St. ☎ 905.356.2651 🖱 skylon.com) The itty bitty baby brother to the world-famous Canada's National Tower in nearby Toronto, Skylon Tower does have what Toronto's otherwise superior counterpart doesn't: the best view from land of all three Niagara Falls. The total height of the tower is 520 feet, but the drop to the Niagara River in the Great Gorge is 775 feet (CN Tower is 1,815 feet, the tallest building in the world.

Visitors take one of the "Yellow Bug" elevators up to the top of the tower. These elevators are glass-enclosed and ride along the exterior of the tower, so the ascent to the observation deck is a thrill itself. At the top, visitors may walk around inside or outside on a special viewing platform that winds all the way around. There is also a gift shop at the top, and two restaurants that give breathtaking panoramic views of the entire Niagara region, with visibility sometimes up to 80 miles on a clear day. Since the tower may be open after dark, lucky visitors will be able to see the fireworks and illumination of the falls. When you are done at the top, the base of Skylon has a small shopping center with unique gift-type shops, and some family-oriented attractions such as **SkyQuest**. *($$)*

KONICA MINOLTA TOWER
(🇨🇦 6732 Fallsview Blvd. ☎ 800.461.2492

🌐 niagaratower.com) Clustered among the Fallsview-area hotels is this most recognizable building: The Konica Minolta Tower. It's a bit fatter and shorter than the nearby **Skylon Tower**, but it has some interesting features. For one thing, there is the **The Tower Hotel** on the top. Although the hotel only has about 40 rooms, they are all 500 feet above the falls, and some of the rooms have breathtaking views.

Also atop the tower is a restaurant and lounge, **The Pinnacle**. There is an observation deck as well, for visitors who would like to see the view but who aren't interested in eating or staying in the tower. *($)*

MUSEUMS AND LEARNING CENTERS

In addition to the myriad educational activities offered by the Niagara Parks, there are many places in town (on both sides of the falls) to learn about Niagara's history and nature.

IMAX NIAGARA

(🍁 6170 Fallsview Blvd. ☎ 905.374.IMAX

🖱 imaxniagara.com) IMAX movies, a technology made in Canada, are the most famous large-format movies. They play on screens much bigger than standard films. Some IMAX theaters play rotating movies (such as Hollywood feature films enlarged for large-screen presentation), and others, like the IMAX Niagara, play only specific movies, mostly sweeping and visually rich documentaries. IMAX documentaries in general tend to convey little information, but make up for it with high-quality landscape images, which many times may make visitors feel like they are flying.

The resident **IMAX Theatre** in Niagara Falls has been playing the same film for several years now. It is *Niagara: Miracles, Myths, and Magic*. The hour-long movie showcases highlights of the history of Niagara Falls. It focuses on the modern development of the region, including some of the more dramatic human encounters. Much of it consists of re-enactments of famous events and sweeping panoramic views and fly-through shots.

Also at the complex is the **Niagara Daredevil Exhibit**, which has photographs from famous daredevil attempts, as well as some of the actual barrels and contraptions that brought these daredevils over the falls. **The National Geographic Store** is also here, with videos, gifts, and other such merchandise. *($$)*

NIAGARA GORGE DISCOVERY CENTER

(▤ **Niagara Falls State Park** ☎ **716.278.1070**) Located on the opposite end of the **Niagara Falls State Park** from Goat Island is the Niagara Gorge Discovery Center. Here is where visitors can learn all about the geology of the falls and the Great Gorge, including historical presentations, and exhibits, and even a movie. *($)*

DAREDEVIL MUSEUM

(▤ **303 Rainbow Blvd.** ☎ **716.282.4046**) Relics, remnants, and photographs of Niagara's star-stunt-ed past are immortalized in this small but thorough museum. Here, visitors learn about some of man's – and woman's – famous attempts to brave Niagara Falls – be it in a barrel, with a jet ski, or even with nothing at all. Among the exhibits are actual devices used by the daredevils as they made the plunge. Visitors can learn the amazing stories of those who survived their attempts, and those who did not. *($)*

NIAGARA'S WAX MUSEUM OF HISTORY

(▤ **303 Prospect St.** ☎ **716.285.1271**) In Niagara Falls, it is indeed strange to visit a wax museum that actually focuses on Niagara Falls. At Niagara's Wax Museum, walk through several scenes of historic Niagara, including street scenes, people of the Niagara Frontier, and even a depiction of the dumping scow rescue; this museum is packed with representations of Niagara's past. Visitors learn about daredevils, electricity, famous events, famous people, and more.

The wax museum is a bit old and less "flashy" than those on Clifton Hill, but it focuses very specifically on the events that shaped the region. A visit to this quiet museum open year-round is well worth it for any visitors walking around the American side. *($)*

NIAGARA AEROSPACE MUSEUM
(⬛ 345 Third St. ☎ 716.278.0060 ♨ niagaramuseum.org)
Aviation enthusiasts are likely aware of the important role played by western New York state during the dawn of aviation. The Niagara Aerospace Museum pays tribute to aviation in the area, and has several full-size planes on display, as well as exhibits highlighting many facets of aviation for the greater Niagara region. *($)*

LUNDY'S LANE HISTORICAL MUSEUM
(🍁 5810 Ferry St. ☎ 905.358.5082 ♨ lundyslanemuseum.com)
Don't let the name fool you – unlike the "other" museums (wax museums) in this area, the Lundy's Lane Historical Museum is owned by the City of Niagara Falls. Here, the focus is Niagara Falls history. Many artifacts are present in this two-story building, erected in 1874 as the Town Hall of Stamford. The exhibits herein include remnants of the Battle of 1812, old postcards and photographs, and the Queen Victoria Fountain. The museum's environment is subdued and peaceful, with displays covering many facets of the Niagara region's history.

The Lundy's Lane Historical Museum is the "main" branch of three museums run by the City of Niagara Falls Board of Museums. Additionally, the **Willoughby Historical Museum** *(9935 Niagara Parkway)* has other items of Niagara-esque historical interest – including genealogy. The **Battle Ground**

Hotel Museum *(6151 Lundy's Lane)* is located on part of the old Lundy's Lane Battlefield, where some of the most violent fighting during the War of 1812 took place. The museum has replicas of rooms and taverns, the way they looked during the days of early tourism (about the 1850s). *($)*

MACKENZIE PRINTERY & NEWSPAPER MUSEUM

(🍁 1 Queenston St., Queenston ☎ 905.262.5676

🍴 mackenzieprintery.ca) A short distance from Niagara Falls the Mackenzie Printery & Newspaper Museum offers visitors the chance to learn about historical newspaper production in Ontario. While the subject matter is strictly Canadian, the museum contains many historical technologies and practices. William Lyon Mackenzie, for whom the museum is named, started publishing the *Colonial Advocate* newspaper in 1824 and was the first mayor of Toronto. He later became a major player during the Upper Canada Rebellion of 1837. With the help of the Niagara Parks Commission, the restored museum opened to the public in 1991. The museum is only open seasonally, so visitors should contact the place in advance for details about visiting hours. *($)*

ANIMALS AND WILDLIFE

Though Niagara Falls is far from the natural animals-roam-free environment that is was thousands of years ago, its prime attraction is natural – and it shows in the area's high-quality exhibits of animals, birds, insects, and more. Many of these exhibits are world famous, almost as popular as the falls themselves.

AQUARIUM OF NIAGARA

(▤ 701 Whirlpool St. ☎ 716.285.3575

⬤ aquariumofniagara.org) Since its opening in 1965, the Aquarium of Niagara has become one of the more popular attractions on the American side of the falls with locals as well as tourists. The facility houses some 1,500 different species of marine life, including sea lions, sharks, penguins, and many kinds of fish. The exterior mural – painted by marine artist Wyland – features a large whale. From the observation deck, visitors can see Horseshoe Falls in the distance. The aquarium is open year-round. *($)*

BUTTERFLY CONSERVATORY

(🇨🇦 2405 Niagara River Pkwy. ☎ 905.358.0025

⬤ niagaraparks.com) Continuously rated one of the best attractions at Niagara Falls, the famous Butterfly Conservatory is a world within itself. Year-round, visitors step out of Canada and into a tropical rainforest swarming with life. As they walk through the winding paths of the indoor environment, natural life abounds. Butterflies flutter everywhere. From common to exotic, from large to small, butterflies are everywhere. This is an extremely popular attraction and will be crowded during the peak summer months. The Butterfly Conservatory is located within the Niagara Falls **Botanical Gardens** facility. *($)*

NIAGARA FALLS AVIARY/BIRD KINGDOM ✪ Must See!

(🇨🇦 5651 River Rd. ☎ 905.356.8888

⬤ niagarafallsaviary.com) Opened in 2003, the Niagara Falls Aviary is one of the newest attractions in Niagara Falls – and it is also one of the best. Home to the largest indoor aviary in the world, the "lost kingdom" theme takes visitors into a forbidden world of ancient ruins with over 300 exotic birds. Some are caged, but others fly freely around the atrium, and visitors may even be able to approach them.

This is a truly impressive attraction. Visitors are encouraged to freely roam the atrium's winding paths and enjoy the lush jungle environment (complete with a waterfall) as they identify the many birds around them. Located immediately off the Rainbow Bridge, the aviary is open year-round, and is frequently crowded. *($$)*

HORSE PLAY NIAGARA

(|✚| Hwy. #3 ☎ 905.834.2380 ☗ horseplayniagara.com) About 25 minutes away from Horseshoe Falls is a genuine horse-riding experience. Beginners and veterans alike can ride atop a horse on one of several excursions, ranging from an hour to all day. Experiences can be trail rides, guided tours, and more. They will cater to your various requirements, and regularly accommodate large groups such as school outings. This is a true horseback-riding experience.

This facility is rather out of the way, located west of Port Colborne on Highway # 3. Contact them for specific directions. (Limited Seasonal) *($$/$$$)*

GOLF COURSES

The entire Niagara region is chock-full of golf courses, both public and private. Niagara Falls itself is home to several of these courses, with skill levels and sizes ranging the gamut of professional and amateur limits. The Niagara Parks Commission owns and manages some of these courses. Following is a list of select *public* golf courses within the Niagara Falls area. The operating hours of these courses tends to be seasonal.

LEGENDS ON THE NIAGARA

(🍁 9233 Niagara Pkwy. ☎ 866.465.3642

🖱 niagaraparksgolf.com) A Niagara Parks offering, Legends on the Niagara features not one, but three golf courses. The 18-hole **Battlefield Golf Course** is situated right next to the site of an important battle during the War of 1812. One particular hole offers a distant view of Niagara Falls. Just south, the **Ussher's Creek Golf Course** offers an additional 18 holes of play through a serene wooded environment. The 9-hole **Chippawa Golf Course** is designed for shorter games, and is frequently used for practice rounds. All courses of Legends on the Niagara have sand traps, banks, creeks and/or lakes, and many of the standard obstacles to overcome.

WHIRLPOOL GOLF COURSE

(🍁 3351 Niagara Pkwy. ☎ 905.356.1140 🖱 whirlpoolgolf.com) The Whirlpool Golf Course is an 18-hole golf course set against the Whirlpool Rapids area of the Niagara River. It is part of the Niagara Parks' series of golf courses. The course caters to customers both professional and amateur, and there is a range of amenities available to help improve one's golf game. There is an on-site restaurant and pro shop.

OAK HALL GOLF CLUB

(🍁 7400 Portage Rd. ☎ 905.358.6418

🖱 niagaraparksgolf.com) The smallest course in the Niagara Parks' roster is the Oak Hall Golf Course. A 9-hole par 3, the course is smaller than the rest, and the holes are shorter and easier. Oak Hall is popular with novice and fair-weather golfers. If you just want to have fun on an easier Niagara Parks course, Oak Hall is a good choice.

BEECHWOOD GOLF & COUNTRY CLUB
(I✦I 4680 Thorold Townline Rd. ☎ 905.680.4653
🖰 beechwoodgolf.com) The Beechwood Golf & Country club had 18 professional holes, and the clubhouse has facilities for all kinds of dining and banquet experiences – even weddings and receptions.

ROLLING MEADOWS GOLF & COUNTRY CLUB
(I✦I 12741 Montrose Rd. ☎ 905.384.9894
🖰 rollingmeadows.ca) This 18-hole professional golf course is known for its unusually steep slope. The clubhouse features a nice variety of snack delights and full-fledged meals.

CASINOS

Niagara Falls is home to three casinos; one on the American side and two on the Canadian side. While most of the attractions cater to summer guests, the casinos enjoy year-round customers.

Within some national legal boundaries, casino gambling in Canada today is under the control of the individual provinces. Within the provinces, however, there is tight control over the industry – it is far from a free market. In fact, except for some private contractors, it is largely a government-run industry.

In the United States, the **Seneca Gaming Corporation** (🖰 *senecagamingcorporation.com*) operates two casinos in the Buffalo/Niagara Falls area; the other being the **Seneca Allegany**

Casino. This is an odd juxtaposition of casinos that exist only a short distance from each other; right across the river. On one side, the government controls and owns the casinos. On the other side, casino gambling is outlawed altogether – so it is under Native American control.

Important: You may (and probably will) lose money when you gamble. *You must be at least 19 years old to gamble in Ontario, or at least 21 years old to gamble in New York.*

NIAGARA FALLSVIEW CASINO ✪ Must See!
(🍁 6380 Fallsview Blvd. ☎ 888.FALLSVUE

🖰 fallsviewcasinoresort.com) Fallsview Casino's floor is about 180,000 square feet and features about 3,000 slot machines and 150 table games, including many of the favorites. For regular (that is, frequent) players, Fallsview offers the **PAC** (Players Advantage Club) where you can earn casino comps. The casino is open 24 hours a day, seven days a week, and you must be 19 to enter the casino floor.

In addition to the casino, Fallsview Casino has a regular array of headlining entertainment in its resident **Avalon Ballroom**. Tickets are available at the ballroom's box office or through TicketMaster *(☎ 877.833.3110 🖰 ticketmaster.com).* This is the main entertainment venue at Fallsview, and one of the larger entertainment arenas in Niagara Falls.

For a more spontaneous evening of entertainment (albeit in a smaller venue), **The 365 Club** also features live acts of various sorts, from musical to comedy and even jam sessions. Also, the **Splash Bar** features smaller live acts on select evenings, where you can listen while you enjoy a drink in a more intimate setting.

The major shopping area is the **Fallsview Galleria**. It cuts through the center of the resort, and also wraps around one of the edges of a concourse. On the lower level, there is even a small café that leads directly outside to a decent view of the falls.

The shops along the promenade are upscale gift shops in nature, including toys, art, crafts, bathing products, and the like. Such well-known brands as **Swarovski** (where you can purchase fine crystal products and accessories) and **Wyland Galleries** (unique artistic creations) can be found here. For fine jewelry, **Reeds Jewelers** carries a line of precious metals and diamonds of various types and qualities. There is a lot more shopping to do in the galleria than is listed here.

For dining choices, the galleria has some good options. **Asian Pearl** offers Asian cuisine in an upscale environment (it over-looks Niagara Falls). For a more relaxed Asian option, **Crazy Sushi** offers dining at either the noodle bar or at a table.

The 1950s diner-style hamburger chain **Johnny Rockets** is here, which is generally a big hit with families and those desiring a quick bite. **Starbucks** is here for coffee needs, and **Punto Dolce** and **Swiss Fudge** for that sweet tooth. There are other eating choices, too, but let's not forget what every good resort-casino must have: a buffet. At Fallsview Casino, it is the **Grand Buffet**, which is located just off the casino floor.

CASINO NIAGARA
(I◆I 5705 Falls Ave. ☎ 888.946.3255 🖱 casinoniagara.com)

When it opened in 1996, Casino Niagara was the first casino in Niagara Falls, as part of the Ontario Gaming Corporation (later the Ontario Lottery and Gaming Corporation). However, unlike the more recent **Fallsview Casino**, Casino Niagara does not have any accommodations on premises. Because of this, those under legal gambling age are not permitted anywhere on the property. Instead, Casino Niagara relies heavily on its more tourist-heavy location near hotels to attract and house those wishing to utilize the facility's entertainment.

Casino Niagara is located adjacent to the Clifton Hill section of town. The access is generous and parking is available either as valet or inside the self-parking garage. The casino is of course smaller than its cross-town counterpart, with fewer slots and table games. However, as the walking access is a little bit easier from the Clifton Hill area, visitors may feel less confined to the casino.

The main shopping option within Casino Niagara is **Connections**, where visitors can purchase all kinds of Casino Niagara memorabilia.

In terms of eating, the choices here are more abundant. For fine dining at Casino Niagara, their premiere establishment is **Twenty One**. The upscale restaurant features fine seafood, steaks, and an extensive wine list. On select evenings, enjoy live music around the restaurant's piano bar. The other option for a fine-dining experience within Casino Niagara is the **Grand Café**, which overlooks some of the casino floor.

The buffet for Casino Niagara is called **The Market Restaurant**. The buffet features various food stations ranging from pasta, seafood, various meats, and dessert. Visitors can enjoy breakfast, lunch, and dinner at the buffet (based on the time of day they choose to dine).

For a more casual experience, **Perks Café** is a coffee bar with pastries, sandwiches, and other quick bites, and it is open 24 hours a day. For the ultimate in casual, the **Terrace Food Court** offers several fast-food options for a quick snack or easy meal. Additionally, the popular **Hard Rock Café** and **Planet Hollywood** are both adjacent to the casino, for easier access.

SENECA NIAGARA CASINO
(▤ **310 Fourth St. ☎ 877.863.6322**

🖱 **senecaniagaracasino.com**) Niagara Falls, New York has a grand casino resort. The 600-plus room, *AAA Four Diamond* facility features 26 floors, a complete pool and spa facility, performance and trade show venues and, of course, lots of casino gaming space. The resort is owned and managed by the Seneca tribe of Native Americans.

Eating at the Seneca Niagara Casino offers several choices as well. **The Western Door** is the resident steak house, with all kinds of chops, sandwiches, fish, and a wide selection of wines. For more of a casual atmosphere, **Morrie's Place** is a sports restaurant and bar, where patrons can eat a variety of traditional food while they watch one of the establishment's several televisions.

Of course, every good casino must have a buffet. And here, the **Thunder Falls Buffet** offers a variety of high-quality foods on a rotating basis. For the smaller appetites, the **NY Deli** and the **Java Café** offer quick bites and snacks.

Seneca Niagara Casino has a few venues where it hosts regular, ongoing entertainment. The **Bear's Den Showroom** is a rather small concert hall where the performers are almost up close and personal with the audience. For larger events, the **Conference Center Niagara Falls** is not a part of Seneca Niagara's main resort complex, but rather a short walk away. It is here where the larger events take place. Additionally, **Club 101**, located right in the center of the casino, hosts various live events.

AMUSEMENT PARKS

Pay one admission fee and enjoy these parks all day long. The Niagara region has plenty of places where thrilling rides and cotton candy go hand-in-hand. While not all these parks are directly in or at the falls themselves, they are relatively close by and can be enjoyed either for an afternoon or all day. They are all very popular attractions.

MARINELAND
(🇨🇦 7657 Portage Rd. ☎ 905.356.9565

🌐 marinelandcanada.com) The Niagara region's answer to Sea World is the smaller but more spread-out Marineland. The park is a mix of aquarium attractions and rides. Much of it is designed for very young children with their families. There are also several shows on the property that have a regular rotation.

Killer Whales and Beluga Whales are major animal headliners at Marineland. Visitors may be able to visit these animals up close and personal, and even pet them. Those attending one of the shows may see dolphins, sea lions, and walruses. There is a pond where visitors may feed swarming fish, and even a place to meet animals of the land, such as deer and bears.

There are a few standard amusement rides. Of special note is the world's largest steel roller coaster, laid out over 30 acres.

Also enjoy the feeling of being propelled straight upwards at 60 miles per hour on the park's skyscraping tower ride (the tower ride is brilliantly positioned so that anybody viewing Horseshoe Falls can see it on the distant horizon).

Marineland is large but unimpressive, with the attractions spread out over many acres. The parking lot is long and a bit unorganized. Marineland is heavily advertised, so you're interest will no doubt be piqued. However, this is not a recommended attraction. Unless you have very young children intent on seeing aquatic or animal life, you should instead check out **Martin's Fantasy Island** or **Six Flags Darien Lake** instead of Marineland. (Seasonal) *($$$)*

MARTIN'S FANTASY ISLAND ✪ Must See!
(▦ 2400 Grand Island Blvd. ☎ 716.773.7591

🖱 martinsfantasyisland.com) There is a certain kind of home-grown charm to small amusement parks such as this. Martin's Fantasy Island on Grand Island is everything you would expect a small amusement park to be: a clean, family-friendly environment with lots of small rides and a few larger ones. The park is several parks in one: a traditional theme park, a petting zoo, and even a small water park – all of which are included in the single-price admission.

A major wooden roller coaster – the Silver Comet – dominates much of the skyline, but patrons will find on the premises bumper cars, spinning rides, train rides, kiddie rides, and even several small show venues, including a Wild West shootout re-enactment. The small waterpark is attached (accessible directly within the main park) and has slides, a wave pool, and a lazy river.

Martin's Fantasy Island is small and manageable, and packed with midway-type rides. Some areas, such as the "western town" section, are reminiscent of Six Flags; the low admission price may surprise some visitors (only about $25 for the day) and nice selection of attractions. This is a great little park. My favorite attraction: a small pond with canoes equipped with aquatic "training wheels" – even the little ones can paddle without fear of tipping over. (Seasonal) *($$)*

SIX FLAGS DARIEN LAKE
(▦ 9993 Allegheny Rd. ☎ 585.599.4641 🖱 sixflags.com)
Located about 50 miles away from Niagara Falls, Six Flags Darien Lake can be a vacation destination all its own. But with over 30 Six Flags theme parks operating worldwide, chances are good that one of them is nearby. So these parks cater mostly to locals of the Buffalo region. Six Flags parks have become a national staple in world-class amusement parks.

The history of this Darien Lake theme park begins in 1964, when it first opened – as a campground. Through the '60s and '70s, the park began to build attractions around the camping – the first of which were water based. By 1982, it was a full-fledged theme park. After various changes in ownership, Premier Parks acquired Six Flags, and in the 1999 season it became "Six Flags Darien Lake."

Six Flags Parks are known for their roller coasters, and in this capacity Darien Lake satisfies. Visitors will also find many favorites here, such as spinning and churning devices, a raft ride, and countless gift shops and eateries. Darien Lake also features an on-site water park. (Seasonal) *($$$)*

LUNDY'S LANE ATTRACTIONS

[*] Lundy's Lane is a strip of tourist attractions and smaller motels on the Canadian side of the falls that are located out of the main Niagara Falls tourist area, starting about three miles west. Shopping malls, a few go-kart tracks and motels dwindle as visitors drive further away from Niagara Falls and into the Canadian countryside.

SUPER PUTT MINI-GOLF

(7301 Lundy's Lane ☎ 905.354.4916 ♪ superputt.com) In the world of mini-golf courses, this one truly has a unique setting – which is a bit ironic. Most mini-golf courses are built upon themes; pirates, exploration, treasure, and the like. Super Putt, however, has a subdued nature setting, with gently flowing water, flowery gardens, shady trees, and even a gazebo. Super Putt is small – a standard round of 18 holes can take as short as an hour or as long as several hours, depending on how crowded it is. *($)*

NIAGARA GO-KARTS

(7104 Kinsman Court ☎ 905.356.9030 ♪ niagarago-karts.com) Located just off Lundy's Lane, the Niagara Go-Karts fulfills the need for speed. Niagara Falls is not a go-cart kingdom. There aren't many unique tracks to choose from, and the terrain provides little eye candy. However, the go-carts here are touted as being exceptionally fast for their kind. The resident flat track is a little more than half a mile long.

The perfect compliment to a lap around the track – of course – is mini golf. Also on the premises, visitors can putt around all day on 18 holes, surrounded by large plastic animals. The variety of holes and difficulties again isn't up to par with destinations where mini-golf is king (like Myrtle Beach).

The facility may be open off season; call in advance for details if traveling in winter. *($)*

OH CANADA EH? DINNER SHOW

(**8585 Lundy's Lane** ☎ **800.467.2071** 🖱 **ohcanadaeh.com**) The name says it all – it's a comedic tribute to Canada. Pulling out all the stereotypical Canadian punches, *Oh Canada, Eh?* features skits and musical numbers with "Mounties" (Royal Canadian Mounted Police), hockey players, loggers, and more. The songs are familiar Canadian anthems, and the food served is always the same. The show itself is about two hours long and vastly enjoyable. It is basically a comedy musical revue set in the vast wilderness of Canada.

The show has been operating since 1994. In 2002 it became a franchise as a second show opened in the Canadian Rockies. Though the headlining *Oh Canada Eh?* is the main performance throughout the year, there are special shows at certain times of year, such as during the holiday season. *($$$/$$$$)*

NIAGARA GRAND DINNER THEATRE

(**8444 Lundy's Lane** ☎ **905.357.7818** 🖱 **niagaragrand.com**) With an opening in 2001, the Niagara Grand Dinner Theatre boasts regular shows while visitors dine. The theater is located inside the **Americana Conference Resort & Spa**. It is a very small and intimate performance venue – less than 200 seats. Shows are available for both lunch and dinner. The rotation of shows varies depending on the time of year – from family shows and romantic comedies to holiday specials. There is a second theater at the Niagara Parks' **Queenston Heights Restaurant** *(14184 Niagara River Pkwy.)*, which features different shows. *($$$/$$$$)*

CANADA ONE FACTORY OUTLETS

(7500 Lundy's Lane ☎ 905.356.8989

🖱 canadaoneoutlets.com) With about 40 outlets stores along an outdoor shopping mall complex, Canada One is the closest outlet mall to the falls. Most of the stores are popular chains and mall staples, including **Nike, Coach, Tommy Hilfiger,** and **Nine West**. Ample parking is available.

Resorts and Hotels

Niagara Falls features an array of world-class resorts located predominantly on the Canadian side of the falls. Most resorts offer guest rooms featuring sweeping views of the falls, and all of them offer top-notch restaurants and entertainment. The area is not a "resort paradise" like Orlando or Las Vegas, but the opportunity to see one of nature's most romantic awe-inspiring wonders from your room's window makes many of the accommodations very appealing.

With few exceptions, when deciding to stay in Niagara Falls, there are two main schools of thought: are you staying to admire the water, or are you staying to enjoy the other attractions? If you have come to stare at Niagara, you'll be much happier in the **Fallsview** section of town; the hotels there are generally much larger resort-types, with great views of Niagara Falls. If you have come for the other attractions (such as wax museums and theme restaurants), you will probably be better off staying in the **Clifton Hill** section, where the hotels are smaller and more basic, but have great access to the Clifton Hill attractions.

Staying in one section of course does not restrict you to vacation fun only in that section. Clifton Hill and Fallsview are only about a mile apart, so a quick drive or taxi ride will get visitors back and forth with the greatest of ease.

Also note that there is no price guide for the hotels. Prices fluctuate so much day-to-day and month-to-month, sometimes as much as hundreds of dollars, so it is impossible to quantify hotel prices. Your best bet is a relative comparison: staying in a top hotel during the summer will be generally more expensive than staying in an average motel during the winter.

Of course, there are many more overnight accommodations available in Niagara Falls than are listed here, from smaller hotels to independent motels. What follows are among the best and most prominent accommodation options that the city has to offer.

FALLSVIEW AREA RESORTS

From the moment visitors cross the Rainbow Bridge or enter Niagara Falls from the Q.E.W., the staggering resorts of the Fallsview area come into view. These behemoths overlook Horseshoe Falls from atop a hill. Upscale, classy, romantic, and full-service establishments, the Fallsview area resorts are the epitome of the way Niagara Falls is envisioned by millions of visitors. Many resorts in this area have earned the *AAA Four Diamond* rating. With honeymoon suites, upscale restaurants, casino gambling, and, of course, sweeping views of Horseshoe Falls from many guest rooms (including views of the fireworks and falls illuminations on select days), Fallsview is where the upscale, romantic tourist wants to be.

The Fallsview area of Niagara Falls is located along Fallsview Avenue, which provides the best vista of Horseshoe Falls from afar. Walking access to the falls from these hotels is more difficult except during the summer months, when the incline railway is running.

These hotels generally offer two room types: Falls View and City View; with Falls View being the more expensive of the two. Many have swimming pools and some have more elaborate fitness and spa centers. Please call the hotel in advance for more specific information.

NIAGARA FALLSVIEW CASINO ✪ Must See!

(🍁 6380 Fallsview Blvd. ☎ 888.FALLSVUE

🖱 fallsviewcasinoresort.com) The Niagara Fallsview Casino is the newest of the two casino resorts in Niagara Falls, Ontario (it began construction in 2001). It is owned and managed by the Ontario Lottery and Gaming Corporation. It is located in the Fallsview section of Niagara Falls, surrounded mostly by the larger hotels with great views of Horseshoe Falls.

Though the resort offers about 400 rooms of various qualities, visitors don't need to spend the night there to enjoy the other facilities, since so many other hotels are located just steps away (or perhaps across the street). However, guests of the resort have access to a full-service health spa, as well as fitness equipment and an indoor pool. The resort also has two full wedding chapels. These chapels can hold a small wedding party, but they can be combined to hold up to 100 guests. Several wedding packages are available.

HILTON NIAGARA FALLS FALLSVIEW

(6361 Fallsview Blvd. ☎ 905.354.7887 🖱 niagarafallshilton.com) The Hilton Niagara Falls Fallsview is an upscale, full-service resort with many on-property amenities. The resort caters to a surprisingly wide range of people. Of course, it offers breathtaking views of Horseshoe Falls (if you book a "falls view" room). It is one of the most beautiful hotels in Niagara Falls, Ontario.

One of the most prominent complexes in the resort is an indoor water park and fitness facility. Located just off the main lobby, the **Adventure Pool** area features a large swimming pool, a waterslide, waterfall, fitness and spa equipment.

Resorts and Hotels

The **Watermark Restaurant**, located on the upper levels of the resort, is an upscale resort dining experience featuring a menu of steak, seafood, and pasta. The restaurant has an aquatic theme, but the most prominent feature is its panoramic windows and unsurpassed views of Horseshoe Falls.

For grown-up fun, the Hilton is also located directly across the street from the **Niagara Fallsview Casino** with easy access via an indoor walkway.

The staff at the Hilton claims that – at 53 stories – the newest tower of the Hilton is taller than the nearby **Skylon Tower**. It is hard to tell the difference, but standing atop Skylon does seem to put the top windows of the hotel at eye level.

EMBASSY SUITES FALLSVIEW

(6700 Fallsview Blvd. ☎ 905.356.3600

☋ embassysuitesniagara.com) Embassy Suites' signature large rooms are here in Fallsview, featuring a wide range of accommodations and several on-site amenities.

The steakhouse restaurant at Embassy Suites Fallsview is **The Keg**. Like its neighboring resorts, The Keg offers unsurpassed views of Horseshoe Falls while dining. Atmosphere is casual, and the menu offers the expected steak and seafood dishes.

Embassy Suites has a basic indoor pool, hot tubs, and a fitness facility. The resort also boasts that it is the closest one to the falls, but the views aren't necessarily any better. Still, for larger accommodations, views of the falls, and easy access to nearby attractions, Embassy Suites Fallsview is a top choice for visitors.

Resorts and Hotels

FALLSVIEW PLAZA HOTEL

(6455 Fallsview Blvd. ☎ 905.357.5200 🖱 fallsviewhotel.com)
The Fallsview Plaza offers a wide array of rooms and suites, including suites with hot tubs. Just off the lobby, **East Side Mario's** offers Italian food in a more relaxed environment.

The resort is directly across the street from the **Niagara Fallsview Casino**. The large pool and fitness facility pales in comparison to the Hilton's next door, but still offers up some nice relaxation. Though the hotel does offer views of the falls, the best attraction here is its close proximity to the casino.

RADISSON HOTEL AND SUITES FALLSVIEW

(6733 Fallsview Blvd. ☎ 905.356.1944 🖱 niagarafallsview.com)
The Radisson Hotel offers various rooms and suites, some overlooking Horseshoe Falls. There is also an indoor pool, fitness facility, and business and meeting services. For dining on-site, Radisson features a **Tony Roma's** restaurant, which serves meaty dishes in a very casual environment.

SHERATON FALLSVIEW HOTEL

(6755 Fallsview Blvd. ☎ 905.374.1077 🖱 fallsview.com) Not to be outdone by its Clifton Hill counterpart, the Sheraton Fallsview may not be the closest resort to Horseshoe Falls, but it certainly offers some of the best views. Plus its location, slightly behind Horseshoe Falls, allows (in certain rooms) more of a panoramic view of the surrounding Niagara River. The resort features about 400 rooms and a variety of suites. The resort has an indoor swimming pool and fitness facility. On-property restaurants include **A Cut Above**, a casual steakhouse, and **La Piazza**, serving a variety of comfort foods. **Stanley's Lounge** offers drinks and the occasional live entertainment.

THE TOWER HOTEL

(6732 Fallsview Blvd. ☎ 905.356.1501 🖥 niagaratower.com) Located on the top of the **Konica Minolta Tower**, the Tower Hotel is a small but well-situated hotel. With only 42 rooms, it has limited on-property amenities, but visitors enjoy nearby access to the dining and entertainment in the rest of the tower.

Some rooms at The Tower offer amazing views of the falls, with great floor-to-ceiling windows. If you don't have a falls view room, however, the hotel is just average and the rooms are small.

NIAGARA FALLS MARRIOTT FALLSVIEW

(6740 Fallsview Blvd. ☎ 905.357.7300 🖥 niagarafallsmarriott.com) The Marriott Fallsview offers about 430 rooms and a variety of suites. Many rooms overlook Horseshoe Falls. The **Terrapin Grille** offers casual contemporary cuisine overlooking the falls. For casino patrons, the resort offers easy access to the **Fallsview Casino** complex.

There are many choices of room styles at the Fallsview Marriot. Fireplaces, Jacuzzis, and lofted beds are part of the room choices available. The falls view rooms offer floor-to-ceiling windows and unobstructed views. The hotel is also one of the closest to the **Incline Railway**, which (during the tourist season) offers visitors very easy access to **Table Rock** and the attractions by the falls.

The resort also features an indoor pool and recreation facility, which includes a video arcade, a fitness center, and several Jacuzzis. The **Serenity Spa**, a signature on-property attraction, offers a range of classic spa treatments and packages.

DOUBLETREE RESORT LODGE AND SPA

(6039 Fallsview Blvd. ☎ 905.358.3817 🖰 doubletree.com) While still in the Fallsview area, the Doubletree does not offer the kind of sweeping views of Horseshoe Falls that most other area resorts do (though some rooms have views of American Falls). However, Doubletree makes up for this deficiency by offering a superb relaxing atmosphere, a full-featured spa, and other luxurious amenities.

The lobby of the Doubletree is grand, with high ceilings and a second-floor balcony, which offers a feeling of a luxurious National Parks resort. The on-site **AVEDA Day Spa** is full-featured. Prominent relaxation features include several smaller indoor pools, a video arcade, and fitness facilities.

Buchanans restaurant offers continental food choices in an upscale yet casual atmosphere. **Moose & Squirrel** serves coffee and snack food items.

The Doubletree is also well situated. Although it lacks the sweeping views of its at-the-brink neighbors, it is easily accessible from both the Clifton Hill and the Fallsview areas. There isn't much around the hotel, but a short walk is all it takes to experience most of the Niagara Falls attractions.

THE OAKES HOTEL

(6546 Fallsview Blvd. ☎ 905.356.4514 ✆ oakeshotel.com) By far the best feature of The Oakes is its location. Like the other major Fallsview hotels, it offers great views of the falls. There is also a small on-site indoor pool and an observation deck on the 14th floor. The Oakes is sandwiched between much larger and plusher hotels, but for those on a budget who still want a falls view room, this may be a good choice.

CLIFTON HILL AREA HOTELS

Clifton Hill and the intersecting Victoria Avenue are where much of the roadside-style attractions are located, and so the traditional "resort experience" is not a main focus. The area has a few guest rooms with great views of the American Falls, but the attractions here are not devoted to the falls. Visitors with a desire to be close to bustling activity, restaurants, bars, and clubs, will be right at home staying here.

The hotels here are generally smaller and more budget-friendly than the hotels in the Fallsview section, with fewer on-site amenities. However, keep in mind that the prime Clifton Hill location is the main draw here. Also, easy walking access to American Falls, **Maid of the Mist**, and the Rainbow Bridge are also big reasons to stay in this popular area.

TRAVELODGE CLIFTON HILL

(4943 Clifton Hill ☎ 905.357.4330 ✆ falls.com) In and of itself, the Travelodge Clifton Hill is about as far from a resort as a hotel can get. It is motel style (guest rooms open to a very noisy parking lot) and there are minimal amenities on-site, including one small outdoor pool. It is located directly on Clifton Hill, within walking distance to **Casino Niagara** and all Clifton Hill attractions.

THRIFTLODGE NIAGARA FALLS

(4945 Clifton Hill ☎ 905.357.4330 🌐 falls.com) Like its neighboring property, **Travelodge Clifton Hill**, the Thriftlodge Niagara Falls is of itself far from a resort, and like its neighbor, it is located on Clifton Hill, within walking distance of **Casino Niagara** and all Clifton Hill attractions. There is an outdoor pool on property.

COMFORT INN CLIFTON HILL

(4960 Clifton Hill ☎ 905.358.3293 🌐 niagarafallscomfort.com) Directly on Clifton Hill, this mid-range hotel offers almost unsurpassed walking access to most Clifton Hill/American Falls attractions. The property features an indoor pool and is located in the middle of the busy tourist district. The resort offers almost no on-site amenities, but many restaurants are located in the immediate vicinity.

SHERATON ON THE FALLS ✪ Must See!

(5875 Falls Ave. ☎ 905.374.4445) Sheraton on the Falls has the distinguished position of being one of Niagara Falls' best resorts, despite being located right in the midst of the kitschy theme park atmosphere of Clifton Hill. The entire **Falls Avenue** complex, including **Casino Niagara**, **Adventure City**, and **Fallsview Indoor Waterpark** can be accessed from Sheraton without ever stepping foot outside. However, unlike the rest of Clifton Hill, the resort is a quiet and luxurious oasis, having earned the *AAA Four Diamond* rating. It is by far the most comprehensive and luxurious resort in Clifton Hill. This hotel mirrors the resorts in the Fallsview section of town, with its sky-scraping architecture and wide array of amenities.

CROWNE PLAZA HOTEL

(5685 Falls Ave. ☎ 800.263.7135 📍 crowneplaza.com) In a neighborhood filled with modern flash, the juxtaposition of the more classically appointed Crowne Plaza (formerly "Brock Plaza") is both puzzling and refreshing. Just off Rainbow Bridge, this is one of the few hotels in Clifton Hill that gives you a (limited) view of Niagara Falls. The hotel has been around since the mid-20th century, and the rooms are smaller but more classically and elegantly decorated. For dining, the **Rainbow Room Fallsview Restaurant** offers continental cuisine and views of the American and Horseshoe Falls.

The main draw of the Crowne Plaza is its prime location. The hotel offers easy indoor access to **Casino Niagara** (it is, in fact the closest hotel to the casino), the **Fallsview Indoor Waterpark**, **Adventure City**, and the rest of the **Falls Avenue** entertainment complex. The hotel does also feature an indoor pool of its own.

SKYLINE INN

(4800 Bender ☎ 800.263.7135 📍 niagarafallshotels.com/skyline) As a "sister" property to the **Crowne Plaza Hotel** and **Falls Avenue** area, Skyline Inn is a smaller motel style property just off the Clifton Hill strip and without views of the falls from guest rooms. However, it offers easy access to both **Casino Niagara** (across the street) and **Fallsview Indoor Waterpark** (via an indoor walkway). Plus, guests enjoy the relative seclusion and easy accessibility to the American Falls and area attractions. In general, the hotel has an old, aged feeling about it, which is charming, but suggests an imminent need for renovation.

DAYS INN & SUITES BY THE FALLS

(5068 Centre St. ☎ 905.357.2550 🖱 daysbythefalls.com) Days Inn by the Falls has the advantage of being close enough to Clifton Hill to practically hear loud commotion – but without being knee-deep in tourists. Otherwise, it's pretty standard. The indoor pool area is nice, but the rooms are small and the décor is a bit tacky. Nonetheless, it's a solid choice for those loyal to the Days Inn brand and who want to stay near Clifton Hill.

STERLING INN & SPA ✪ Must See!

(5195 Magdalen St. ☎ 289.292.0000 🖱 sterlingniagara.com) This little gem is well hidden but still within close walking distance of much of the Clifton Hill attractions – look for the milk bottle-shaped entrance just off Victoria Avenue. The new Sterling Inn – which really used to be a milk bottling facility – bills itself as the only boutique hotel in Niagara Falls; it is modern, fresh, sharp, and a unique addition to the otherwise motel-style hotels of the area.

Sterling Inn is reminiscent of classic New York City boutique hotels – dark ambience, contemporary decorations, spic-and-span rooms and hallways, and a very attentive staff. The rooms themselves (there are less than 50 rooms) are each unique, with wood floors and comfy, modern furniture; some have hot tubs in various configurations. The on-site restaurant, **AG**, is worthy of note on its own. Located in the basement, it features fish and meat dishes, and an extensive wine list. The spa is also in the basement, and features massages and other standard treatments.

The only two things missing at Sterling Inn are a view of the falls, and a swimming pool – but guests are allowed to use the pool at the neighboring **Days Inn**.

COURTYARD BY MARRIOTT

(5950 Victoria Ave. ☎ 905.358.3083 ⏾ nfcourtyard.com) One of the best Courtyard hotels in the Marriott system, this hotel offers the best of both worlds; it is almost exactly in between the Clifton Hill area and the Fallsview area – an easy walk is all it takes to get to most of what Niagara Falls offers. Many guest rooms have faux fireplaces, which can be "ignited" with a light switch. Ten floors make this hotel visible from the American side, yet unfortunately it lacks good views of the falls (a few rooms have limited views). Nonetheless, it is very clean, has an attentive staff, and the location for a well-rounded Niagara Falls vacation is all but unbeatable.

This Courtyard features two pools – one indoors and one outdoors – as well as a hot tub and sauna. The seasonal outdoor pool has a small waterslide. An attached restaurant, **The Keg**, is a basic steakhouse, which doubles as the **Courtyard Café** during breakfast.

AMERICAN-SIDE HOTELS

Since the American side of the falls is less centralized, with fewer attractions, the hotels here are lesser in number. However, they also tend to be less expensive, with comparable amenities.

Most hotels on the American side are concentrated around the Rainbow Bridge, **Seneca Niagara Casino**, and the **Niagara Falls State Park**. These hotels tend to be smaller, with limited amenities but good access to American-side attractions.

CROWNE PLAZA NIAGARA FALLS ✪ Must See!

(300 3rd St. ☎ 716.285.3361 ☷ crowneplaza.com/niagarafalls)
The new Crowne Plaza in downtown Niagara Falls is a great example of neighborhood revitalization. Newly renovated in 2007, smaller motels, neighborhood parking lots, and local businesses surround it. By contrast, the hotel is a unique surprise. It is clean, modern, and spacious, with quality amenities typically associated with hotels on the Canadian side. While staying here doesn't provide you with easy access to the falls, it does offer an alluring alternative – the **Seneca Niagara Casino**, which is next door (across the street). Of course, if you still plan on exploring the falls, they are only a short walk (or even shorter taxi ride) away.

There is a casual restaurant on property, the **Old Falls Sports Bar & Grille**, which offers casual food and beer at inflated prices. There is a nice indoor pool and fitness center on the property, as well as a small video arcade and gift shop. However, the casino next door has many other dining and entertainment options. The prices at the casino aren't any better, but there are more choices. It is nice to have access to the casino's amenities but without the pressure to gamble.

It is unfortunate that no hotel on the American side offers jaw-dropping views of the falls, so other amenities are a must. That said, the Crowne Plaza is the best Niagara Falls hotel on the American side.

Resorts and Hotels

SENECA NIAGARA CASINO RESORT ✪ Must See!
(310 Fourth St. ☎ 877.863.6322 📟 senecaniagaracasino.com)
Niagara Falls, New York has a grand casino resort – the
Seneca Niagara Casino Resort. This 600-plus room, *AAA
Four Diamond* facility features 26 floors, a complete pool and
spa facility, performance and trade show venues, and of course,
lots of casino gaming space. The resort is owned and managed
by the Seneca tribe of Native Americans.

COMFORT INN – "THE POINTE"
(1 Prospect Pointe ☎ 716.284.6835 📟 comfortinnthepointe.com)
The Pointe offers just about the best view of the falls as one
can get from the American side. Though you can't really see
the falls at all, if you manage to secure the right room, you
can get a great view of the American Rapids and the mist of
Horseshoe Falls in the distance.

HOLIDAY INN DOWNTOWN NIAGARA FALLS
(114 Buffalo Ave. ☎ 716.285.2521 📟 holidayinn.com) The
Niagara Falls Holiday Inn is within easy walking distance
of the **Niagara Falls State Park**, which is this hotel's best
feature. The spacious lobby is attached to an enclosed pool
area. As a nice touch, the guest rooms have wooden floors (not
carpet), making them appear more spacious than they actually
are. Some rooms offer views of the state park. This is one of
the better hotels on the American side.

HOWARD JOHNSON CLOSEST TO THE FALLS
(454 Main St. ☎ 716.285.5261 📟 hojoniagarafalls.com) Basic
and small, the Niagara Falls HoJo seems to be showing its age.
The rooms are small and the furniture and bedding feels old.

According to the hotel staff, the indoor pool is the only one in Niagara Falls, New York that requires a lifeguard to be on duty due to its depth and its steep underwater slope. Of course, this limits the pool's hours of operation. The hotel is close to the Rainbow Bridge but with very few attractions nearby.

QUALITY HOTEL & SUITES NIAGARA FALLS

(240 First St. ☎ 716.282.1212 ⬤ qualityniagarafalls.com) The Quality Hotel is located on an awkward street corner (where Rainbow Blvd. and First St. diverge) with little to see, so while it is close to the falls, it is hard to tell from the property. While location is by far the best draw, this hotel is small (only four stories). The small, glass-enclosed pool area on the first floor overlooks an unimpressive street. **Legends Bar & Grill** is located on-site, with basic burgers-and-fries offerings. The guest rooms are basically nice, but – like many accommodations in the area – the hotel seems to be showing its age.

DAYS INN NIAGARA AT THE FALLS

(443 Main St. ☎ 716.284.8801 ⬤ daysinn.com) The closest hotel to the Rainbow Bridge on the American side is this Days Inn. It's an impossible hotel to miss – anybody traveling to Canada will pass this antiquated nine-story hotel. It's the last impression visitors see before entering Canada. Rooms are tiny but relatively comfortable, and a small indoor pool is available on the ground floor. Unfortunately, like the nearby Howard Johnson, there is little to see or do in this area; the falls are south of the Rainbow Bridge and this hotel is on the north side. A **Denny's** restaurant is attached to the hotel.

INDOOR WATERPARK RESORTS

The indoor waterpark resort is a year-round family vacation destination generally found in colder northern regions that center on water activities and various other family-friendly activities, such as video arcades.

Please note that that the **Crowne Plaza**, **Skyline Inn**, and **Sheraton on the Falls** at Clifton Hill may also be considered "indoor waterpark resorts" because of their proximity to the **Fallsview Indoor Waterpark**. They are close to the waterpark (and it can be accessed via indoor walkways).

AMERICANA CONFERENCE RESORT & SPA
(|✦| 8444 Lundy's Lane ☎ 905.356.8444

☗ americananiagara.com) The Americana Resort has taken advantage of the recent (and ever-growing) trend of indoor waterparks by building the first one in Niagara Falls. Granted the distinction is short-lived as more are on the way, but nonetheless credit is due for this first step.

The resort is small and motel style and has undergone a renovation that includes **Waves**, the indoor waterpark. The complex is small for such an attraction – only 25,000 square feet – but it delivers the goods: several waterslides, a wave pool and kiddie pool, and even a nearby video arcade. The waterpark is open to the public; however, staying at the resort comes with a certain number of free admissions (day visitors must pay). It is a family place, so expect lots and lots of kids.

In addition to the headlining waterpark, the resort features a spa, a restaurant, and even some during-dinner entertainment:

The **House of Comedy** and the **Niagara Grand Dinner Theatre** – enjoy live performances while you enjoy your food. The resort is also set up for conferences, banquets, trade shows, weddings, and other larger organized activities.

GREAT WOLF LODGE ✪ Must See!
(🇨🇦 3950 Victoria Ave. ☎ 800.605.WOLF 🖱 greatwolflodge.com)
In Niagara Falls, the Great Wolf Lodge has teamed up with **Ripley's Entertainment** to create one of the best family destinations in the Niagara region. Though the Great Wolf Lodge is about two miles from most Niagara Falls attractions, the resort brings such a wide array of superb entertainment options right on the massive complex that its worth the trek outside of the tourist area.

There are a growing number of Great Wolf Lodge resorts in cold-climate vacation towns all across America. The first resort was built in Wisconsin Dells, and now they are in locations such as Williamsburg, Virginia, and Traverse City, Michigan, with more on the way. These resorts share lots of the same characteristics, including the attractions and facilities available. The Great Wolf Lodge is an all-suite hotel designed specifically for families with young children, and as a result, there are lots and *lots* of families with young children.

Of course, the waterpark is the main and largest attraction at Great Wolf Lodge. The 103,000-square-foot waterpark is open year-round, the water is heated, and they have an abundance of watery wonders, including slides, pools, aquatic playgrounds, and such. Waterpark admission is included with the cost of a room. Also on-site are a seasonally open outdoor waterpark, mini-golf, the **Northern Lights Arcade**, and numerous dining and shopping options. The on-site **Elements AVEDA** spa offers a wide range of spa and massage treatments.

Select Restaurants

Niagara Falls is not known for culinary excellence. With few exceptions, the restaurants cater more to their vistas (many claim "fallsview" dining rooms) than to their menus. Nevertheless, Niagara Falls' restaurant selection covers as wide a range as the attractions themselves. If you want a quick bite at your favorite fast food or chain establishment, you will find many to your liking. If you want a quiet, secluded romantic dinner, you will find many more to your liking.

There are restaurants everywhere in Niagara Falls, many within area hotels, both in New York and Ontario. However, the vast majority of the restaurants is in Ontario, and likewise, the select listing of establishments here reflects this heavy majority.

This section lists the more upscale, traditional Niagara Falls dining experiences. For a list of the more "fun" eats, such as theme restaurants on Clifton Hill, see the Fun Eating section of the "Clifton Hill" chapter.

Prices for Niagara Falls restaurants listed in this section are as follows: for average entrées less than $15, $; for average entrées between $15 and $50, $$; and for average entrées greater than $30, $$$. Prices are quoted in the country of the restaurant's location.

CANADIAN SIDE RESTAURANTS

Despite the area's general lack of "good" food, there are some diamonds in the rough. And the Canadian side has the most diamonds.

REVOLVING DINING ROOM

(Skylon Tower, 5200 Robinson St. ☎ 905.356.2651
🖱 skylon.com) For visitors desiring one of the most special dining experiences in Niagara Falls, coupled with one of the best views, the Revolving Dining Room on top of the **Skylon Tower** is pretty much the cream of the crop. Featuring a 360-degree revolving restaurant floor 775 feet above Niagara Falls, the views are second to none. The restaurant is family-friendly (for children 12 and over), casual but upscale. The cuisine includes a wide array of French and continental choices, and an extensive wine list. Also, the **Summit Suite Dining Room** features a lunch and dinner buffet. Reservations may be made online. Look for deals for visiting the observation desk when dining here; there may be discounts available. *($$$)*

ELEMENTS ON THE FALLS

(Table Rock Point ☎ 905.354.3631 🖱 niagaraparks.com)
Elements is on the second floor of the **Table Rock** building, and is absolutely the closest one can possibly dine in from Horseshoe Falls in Canada. It is a casual family dining experience, and is especially wonderful if you manage to (luckily) get a window table. The windows are floor-to-ceiling, so most places to will offer at least some of the view. As for the menu, it is a pricey place, serving a mix of pastas, steaks, and stir-fry dishes. Remember; you're there for the ambience, not the food. *($$$)*

QUEENSTON HEIGHTS RESTAURANT

(14184 Niagara Pkwy. ☎ 905.262.4274 🖱 niagaraparks.com)
Near the Queenston-Lewiston Bridge, the Queenston Heights

Restaurant is an upscale dining facility owned by the Niagara Parks Commission. Families are welcome; a children's menu is available. The Queenston Heights Restaurant is also home to a branch of the **Niagara Grand Dinner Theatre**, with a regular rotation of shows. *($$)*

PINNACLE RESTAURANT

(6732 Fallsview Blvd. ☎ 905.356.1501 🖱 pinnacleniagara.com) For those who enjoy dining in high places, the Pinnacle Restaurant on top of the **Konica Minolta Tower** may be for you. Menu choices are continental and, of course, views of Niagara Falls 525 feet below are not in short supply. *($$/$$$)*

MAMA MIA'S RESTAURANT

(5719 Victoria Ave. ☎ 905.354.7471) At the top of Clifton Hill, surrounded by the newer themed restaurants, is Mama Mia's, a Niagara Falls institution for about half a century. Rated as one of the best family restaurants in the city, Mama Mia's boasts a thoroughly Italian menu and local wines. *($$)*

EDGEWATERS TAP & GRILL

(6342 Niagara Pkwy. ☎ 905.356.2217) With great views of both the American and Horseshoe Falls, Edgewaters Tap & Grill has both inside dining and a seasonal patio. *($/$$)*

FINE KETTLE O' FISH

(3641 Portage Rd. ☎ 905.357.3474 🖱 finekettle.com) For a real down-home fish experience, the small chain restaurant, Fine Kettle O'Fish offers a mix of seafood delights, from chowders to shellfish to fish and chips. *($/$$)*

Select Restaurants

CARPACCIO RESTAURANT

(6840 Lundy's Lane ☎ 905.371.2061 ♨ carpacciorestaurant.com)
This upscale Italian-style restaurant features a wide range of pasta and Italian dishes. For wine enthusiasts, it has an extensive selection (300+ kinds) of wines at its wine bar. *($$)*

BETTY'S RESTAURANT

(8921 Sodom Rd. ☎ 905.295.4436 ♨ bettysrestaurant.com)
This is a good, old-fashioned family restaurant with diner-style food. It has a wide variety of all kinds of dishes, but Betty's is particularly famous for its fish and chips selections. It's clean and out of the main city center (in the old Chippawa section of the city), and is a relaxing retreat. *($)*

AFTER HOURS BISTRO

(5470 Victoria Ave. ☎ 905.357.2503 ♨ afterhoursbistro.com)
The very quaint After Hours Bistro features a wide selection of pastas and wines, and has both a bar/lounge area and restaurant. The establishment has regular live entertainment, and special events throughout the year. *($$)*

YUKIGUNI

(5980 Fallsview Blvd. ☎ 905.354.4440 ♨ yukiguni.ca) Just north of the Fallsview section of town is a very popular Japanese restaurant. The menu features a wide variety of Japanese choices, including sushi, tempura, and noodle dishes. *($/$$)*

SECRET GARDEN RESTAURANT

(5827 River Rd. ☎ 905.358.4588 ♨ secretgardenrestaurant.net)
Offering an angled view of the American Falls, Secret Garden Restaurant features a friendly and comfortable atmosphere. On

the menu are selections of fish, meat, and vegetarian dishes, and a children's menu. *($/$$)*

AMERICAN SIDE RESTAURANTS

Most of the restaurants on the American side are not located near the falls themselves, but rather along Niagara Falls Boulevard, Pine Avenue, and a few other major thoroughfares around town. Chain restaurants are abundant, but plan to do some driving if you want to experience the cuisine of Niagara Falls, New York.

THE COMO RESTAURANT

(2220 Pine Ave. ☎ 716.285.9341 ● thecomorestaurant.com)
In business since 1927, the Como Restaurant serves a wide range of casual American and Italian cuisine. Lunch and dinner menus are available. *($/$$)*

LA GALERA

(6621 Niagara Falls Blvd. ☎ 716.283.4274) Just about the best Mexican food one can get in Niagara Falls, New York, La Galera is out of the tourist section of town, along Niagara Falls Boulevard. The décor is average to a little run-down, and the exterior leaves much to be desired. Most diners swear by the food. Some, however, say that it lacks authenticity. *($)*

LA HACIENDA

(3019 Pine Ave. ☎ 716.285.2536) La Hacienda is an old restaurant that has locals and visitors alike raving about its pizza. Sure, they serve more than just pizza here, but pizza is by far the best dish on this menu. The ambience, however, is a bit grimy and leaves a lot to be desired. *($/$$)*

MICHAEL'S

(3011 Pine Ave. ☎ 716.282.4043 ⬤ michaelsniagarafalls.com) Michael's Restaurant is an extremely popular family-friendly Italian restaurant that has blossomed to become a real area hotspot. The food ranges from good to just okay, and the portions can be large (order a half-size pasta dish if you're not extremely hungry). The food is primarily pasta-Italian, but sandwiches, steak, ham, chicken, pizza, and others are available. *($)*

TOP OF THE FALLS RESTAURANT

(Goat Island ☎ 716.278.0337 ⬤ topofthefallsrestaurant.com) This fine-dining establishment is within the Niagara Falls State Park. Dine while you overlook **Terrapin Point** and Horseshoe Falls. *($$)*

HARD ROCK CAFÉ

(333 Prospect St. ☎ 716.282.0007 ⬤ hardrockcafe.com) There is a Hard Rock Café on both sides of the falls. While both offer substantially the same food choices, the location on the Canadian side – on Clifton Hill – is far better. The Hard Rock Café on the American side is almost across the street from the **Niagara Falls State Park**, a short hike from the American Falls. The restaurant serves up greasy burgers, chicken fingers, steaks, and a wide array of drinks while surrounding its visitors with rock 'n' roll artifacts attached to the walls and in display cases. *($$$)*

CAFFE LOLA

(507 Third St. ☎ 718.282.LOLA ⬤ caffelola.com) Operated by a long-time Niagara Falls resident, Caffe Lola is a newer addition to the restaurant offerings on the American side, with some of the tastiest food available in town. On the menu are soups and salads, panini, gnocchi, ravioli, and other staples, all of which are generally light. For dessert, the restaurant specializes in gelato. A kids' menu is available. *($$)*

DONATELLO'S

(466 3rd St. ☎ 716.282.2069) While the inside is in need of some serious renovation (the décor feels dated), the food itself is tasty and relatively inexpensive. The sandwiches and pizza are among the most popular dishes. Donatello's is extremely casual and low-key, and has deli-style service. *($)*

GIGIO'S CAFÉ

(1821 Pine Ave. ☎ 716.282.9144) This is the must-do breakfast place in Niagara Falls, New York, according to many locals. The menu is extensive, and particularly popular on the menu is the Italian sausage. The restaurant feels homey and comfortable. *($)*

Select Restaurants

The flow of water over Niagara Falls is heavily controlled by area hydroelectric power plants.

Clifton Hill

[🍁] In Canada, Clifton Hill is the tinsel epicenter of Niagara Falls. Everything is loud here. With bright lights, huge signs, the background chatter of video arcades, and lots of music coming from every direction, it sparks a fury of activity from its younger visitors. Next to the falls themselves, this is the most popular tourist area in Niagara Falls, and as much of the attractions are indoors, nearly all the facilities here are open year-round. Interestingly enough, the falls are all but non-existent in this part of town.

Clifton Hill begins about a mile north of the falls, at River Road (the road which follows the Niagara River north, past the falls – eventually becoming the Niagara Parkway). Clifton Hill twists upwards on a moderately steep "hill." From River Road, visitors get the best view of the tourist district. From here, the signs are large and colorful (and brightly lit at night), with several famous corporate chains of attractions making their impressions, and each vying for your patronage.

The twist at the top of Clifton Hill makes the tourist area seem bigger than it actually is. The main stretch of tourist commerce is only a few hundred feet up this hill (easily walkable in only a few short minutes). This area is also known as "the center" or "the hill."

Clifton Hill is a mush of things that spreads out beyond the hill itself; the **Falls Avenue** attractions and **Victoria Avenue** attractions (two streets that intersect the hill) are also considered to be part of this area. While visitors could spend the whole day enjoying the restaurants and attractions here, die-hard kitsch fans could blast through all the main attractions in as little as two hours.

HISTORY

Clifton Hill got its name in 1832 by a British Army Officer named Captain Ogden Crieghton. He acquired the land in that area from the Phillip Bender family. With the intention of turning the land into a settlement, Crieghton divided it into lots, designed the street layout, and called the area "Clifton" after a town in England of the same name. He built his own home on a lot overlooking what is now the American Falls.

At the time, the only way to cross the river was with a ferry service. The ferry landing was at the foot of Ferry Road (which would later become the road of "Clifton Hill"). Because there was heavy traffic near the ferry landing, the first hotel was built a year later, at the foot of Ferry Road. This was a large and high-class establishment; the best in the area at the time.

From then, the town grew slowly. In 1842, railway financier Samuel Zimmerman obtained a large portion of land at the foot of Ferry Road and began to build an enormous mansion in which he one day hoped to live. However, he was killed in a railway accident in 1857. A few years later, the unfinished estate was purchased and completed by a senator from New York, John T. Bush. The Bush family lived in the mansion for the next 50 years. Shortly after his death in 1937, the mansion was demolished. At its most expansive, the estate took up nearly all the property from what is present-day Clifton Hill, all the way to the falls (visitors driving along River Road from Clifton Hill to the falls are driving through the estate property). Only a small portion of the mansion exists today – a small fountain pond near the entrance to **Queen Victoria Park**.

But the fate of Zimmerman's mansion was not for naught. He was essential in establishing a railway through the entire Niagara region, which was largely responsible for the trade (and ultimately tourism) that followed. In 1856 the Village of Clifton and nearby Elgin were incorporated into the Town of Clifton, and in 1881 it became the Town of Niagara Falls.

ATTRACTIONS

Visitors looking for tinsel, kitsch, and throngs of tourists – but without any waterfall – needn't venture far. Clifton Hill fills this void and then some. Close enough to **Table Rock Point** to warrant tourist traffic, but far enough away that the noise and bright lights of the strip don't interfere with the noise and bright lights of the falls, Clifton Hill is where one goes at night, or when one has seen enough falling water. Visitors can expect the short strip to be packed to the brim with small, time-consuming enjoyment gadgets.

The attractions here are all located either on Clifton Hill or just off the main strip – they are all easily accessible from each other. As visitors will see, there are a lot of things to do on Clifton Hill, all packed into such a small area.

WAX MUSEUMS

A wax museum is a special kind of museum. It relies not on genuine artifacts to fill the exhibits, but rather replications of artifacts. This opens the door of possible exhibits to a limitless nature. Wax museums come in many shapes and sizes, but they all have one thing in common: they imitate reality. The Clifton Hill area is positively chock-full of wax museums, so lovers of this kind of attraction will be on cloud nine.

Clifton Hill

Wax museums have matured as a cultural phenomenon to become the apex of kitsch. A material swelling with possibilities, wax is both a product and a metaphor. It has the ability to change form with a limit akin only to imagination, yet it is substantially frail and weak. It can look strong but it is not strong. Anything can be made from wax – and that's the beautiful part. Pets, jewelry, cars – even walls or whole rooms, can be imitated in this flexible but flaccid material.

ARCADES AND AMUSEMENTS

Are those quarters burning holes in your pockets? Are you positively aching to be shaken in a darkened theater, or lifted above the buildings for a sweeping panoramic view? Then look no further than Clifton Hill.

EATING AND SHOPPING

Like chains and theme restaurants? Look no further than the plethora of choices along this oh-so-commercial strip. Gift shops and more are also prevalent.

NIGHTLIFE

Clifton Hill fares well at night, especially in the summertime, when the signs are illuminated to their full glory, and the crowds are party-hardy. The restaurants and bars are generally open, and there is much to do. In short, when it is too dark to see the falls, see Clifton Hill instead.

GETTING THERE

Clifton Hill is easily accessible by car from the United States over the Rainbow Bridge. After crossing the bridge into Canada, make your way to River Road heading south. Clifton

Hill will be almost immediately on your right, so follow the signs. There is limited parking on the strip itself, but many of the local hotels and motels provide use of their lots (for a fee). From the Fallsview (Murray Hill) section of town, where many of the larger hotels are, take Fallsview Boulevard to Victoria Avenue, then make a right onto Clifton Hill.

Walking to Clifton Hill is also a possibility – and a highly popular one at that. From **Table Rock Point,** near the foot of the Fallsview section, there is a long and pretty promenade along the river and River Road that takes you almost exactly to the foot of Clifton Hill (expect a 20 minute walk, or longer, from Table Rock Point). There is also public transportation (Niagara Transit) that will take you that same length.

RIPLEY'S ENTERTAINMENT

Even for those who don't typically enjoy walk-through attractions built with odd façades and featuring fascinating facts, goofy gags, and the occasional shrunken head, everybody will find something at Ripley's that will make them smile.

Ripley's chain of museums is large – and they know their market. Wherever there is a vacation town, there seems to be a Ripley's Believe it or Not! Museum. But Ripley's is more than just museums. They operate a "moving theater," mini-golf courses, haunted houses, the Louis Tussaud's and Guinness World Records Museums, and even a growing chain of aquariums.

Robert Leroy Ripley was born in 1890 in Santa Rosa, California. In 1908, he sold his first comic to *LIFE* magazine. After working for the *San Francisco Chronicle* and Boston's *The Globe*, he decided to travel abroad. In 1918, he drew a cartoon featuring

Clifton Hill

sports oddities, and one year later drew a comic called *Believe It Or Not!* From then on, Ripley traveled the world in search of oddities to write about and publish in his comic strips. In 1929 his strips earned syndication, read by millions worldwide. Ripley would work for radio, create short films, and explore different avenues for his *Believe It or Not!* idea. In 1933, the first "Odditorium" museum opened in Chicago, followed shortly thereafter by San Diego and Dallas. In 1949, Robert Ripley collapsed on the set of his television show, and died shortly thereafter.

Robert Ripley has the aura of a real-life Indiana Jones. And his museums are a testament to his odd discoveries, and his life. Ripley's has had a presence in Niagara Falls since the 1950s.

RIPLEY'S BELIEVE IT OR NOT! MUSEUM ✪ Must See!

(4983 Clifton Hill ☎ 905.356.2238 🖱 ripleys.com) Ripley's Believe it or Not! Museum is probably the most well-known wax museum chain. Ever since Robert Ripley began showing off his findings at the first Odditorium in Chicago around the 1930s, the unusual and fascinating artifacts contained in his museums have mesmerized people. The chain of Ripley's museums spans the globe; some artifacts are authentic, but many are replicates. In many circumstances, Ripley's uses wax to show human body conditions, such as the man with the spike through his body, or the man with "4 eyes," or the woman with the stretched neck. All these are staples of the Ripley franchise; and many more can be seen on Clifton Hill. Of course, the classic Ripley videos can be seen here too (the man smoking with his eyes, the bendy man, etc.). *($$)*

Clifton Hill

GUINNESS WORLD RECORD MUSEUM

(4943 Clifton Hill ☎ 905.356.2299 ⬤ guinnessattractions.com)
Of similar interest to the Ripley's museum is the Guinness
World Record Museum. Here, visitors can marvel at unusual
people, places, and things that have set world records
according to the Guinness company. If it's the tallest, the
fastest, the smallest, the most climbed, the biggest, the
hairiest, the most expensive, or even the first, chances are
Guinness has recognized it.

The story of how the Guinness Book of World Records began
is now legendary. In 1951, Sir Hugh Beaver, managing director
of the Guinness Brewery, got into a bar fight over which was
the fastest game bird in Europe. Eventually, Beaver realized
that a book of facts such as this may come in handy. By 1955,
the first *Guinness Book of Records* became available, which shot
to the top of the British Bestseller list. Since then, more than
100 million copies of the regularly updated books have been
sold worldwide. Although they started at one point together,
today there is little tie (at least from a lay marketing stand-
point) between the Guinness Book of World Records and the
Guinness Brewery.

There are several Guinness World Record Experiences – in
San Antonio, Hollywood, Gatlinburg, and internationally in
Copenhagen. In 1995, Ripley's Entertainment acquired the
right to operate and license these attractions. *($$)*

RIPLEY'S 4D MOVING THEATRE

(4893 Clifton Hill ☎ 905.356.2261 ⬤ ripleys.com) Ripley's
Entertainment has another attraction at Clifton Hill: Ripley's
4D Moving Theatre. Similar to the **FX Thrill Ride Theatre**,

Clifton Hill

guests are seated in a theater where the seats move in accordance with the images on screen. Ripley's calls this a 4D attraction – guests will feel rain, wind, and more throughout the experience. Ripley's also has moving theater attractions in Myrtle Beach, South Carolina, and Gatlinburg, Tennessee. *($$)*

LOUIS TUSSAUD'S WAXWORKS

(5907 Victoria Ave. ☎ 905.356.2238 🖱 ripleys.com) In 1949, the first wax museum in Niagara Falls opened on Clifton Hill. It was Louis Tussaud's Waxworks. Unfortunately, the lease ran out in 2000, and it had been closed for a while. Finally acquiring a new location, the museum re-opened in the spring of 2005, courtesy of Ripley's Entertainment. Louis Tussaud's is a portraiture museum (replicas of famous people).

The displays here run the gamut of popular culture and historical figures. The replicas are surprisingly accurate and lifelike. A unique trait to Louis Tussaud's Waxworks from other wax museums in the area is that the wax figures are in "open settings" – they are easily accessible, not in display settings. They can be examined up close, and even carefully touched. *($$)*

WALK-THROUGH ATTRACTIONS

Though Ripley's Entertainment holds some of the most famous names in Wax Museum-ness, there are many other brands of wax museums in the area, making Niagara Falls one of the top destinations in North America (and certainly in Canada) for wax museum lovers. This section details the other walk-through attractions in the Clifton Hill area. Some of them are "wax," whereas some are not. But they all share the "tourist walk-through museum" quality that we all love.

Clifton Hill

Warning: Beware of the Haunted Houses! Clifton Hill haunted houses are scary places! Live actors touch, grab, and even lock unsuspecting visitors into rooms for minutes at a time. People who are used to calmer haunted houses or wax museums – even burly adults and older teens – may be unpleasantly surprised by these legitimately scary attractions.

MOVIELAND WAX MUSEUM OF THE STARS ✪ Must See!

(4960 Clifton Hill ☎ 905.356.3061) A favorite landmark on Clifton Hill is the Movieland Wax Museum of the Stars. This walk-though wax museum takes visitors through a collection of random Hollywood movie set reproductions, complete with wax representation of their cast. See such exhibits as Angelina Jolie as Lara Croft, Jack Nicholson as the Joker, Mel Gibson as William Wallace, and many more, all in rooms designed to look like the movies they were in. Visitors may also make wax impressions of their own hands at the conclusion of the self-guided tour for an additional fee. *($$)*

THE CRYSTAL CAVES

(4967 Clifton Hill ☎ 905.357.9660 ⛨ crystalcaves.ca) The Crystal Caves: A Mirror Maze Adventure is a well-designed but expensive maze of mirrors. Upon entering, the ticket clerk gives each participant a pair of plastic gloves, to keep the mirrors clean and the illusion intact. The maze is not dark and only scary if you fear getting lost. The effect is cool but the price is too steep. *($$)*

ROCK LEGENDS WAX MUSEUM

(5020 Centre St. ☎ 905.354.6255

⛨ rocklegendswaxmuseum.com) Just off the main strip, Clifton Hill becomes Centre Street. This is where Rock Legends

Wax Museum is located. On the same "view the stars" par with Movieland, here visitors can see their favorite rock and other popular music legends almost up close and personal. On display are over 60 figures, including Kurt Cobain, Stevie Wonder, Marilyn Manson, and Little Richard. *($$)*

SCREAMERS HOUSE OF HORRORS

(5930 Victoria Ave. ☎ 905.357.7656 🖱 screamersniagara.com) Screamers is a house of almost total darkness and you have to find your way through the creepy hallways. This walk-through attraction has some interesting visual effects and is quite scary. Of course, you can "chicken out" at any time. *($$)*

NIGHTMARES FEAR FACTORY

(5631 Victoria Ave. ☎ 905.357.FEAR 🖱 nightmares-niagara.com) One of the scariest haunted houses in Niagara Falls, Nightmares Fear Factory is aimed squarely at adults (though there is no age restriction). Weave your way through the dark areas of this walk-through attraction. *($$)*

HOUSE OF FRANKENSTEIN

(4967 Clifton Hill ☎ 905.357.9660) In sharp contrast to the largely upbeat nature of **Movieland** and **Rock Legends**, a nearby attraction takes wax museums into a much scarier domain. The House of Frankenstein intends to scare more than it intends to educate, so enter it with caution. *($)*

CLASSIC IRON MOTORCYCLE MUSEUM

(5473 Victoria Ave. ☎ 905.374.8211 🖱 classiciron.ca) As the name suggests, this museum features a collection of motorcycles of various shapes and sizes, as well as all kinds of motorcycle-related information. Enthusiasts of these vehicles will feel right at home here. *($$)*

THE HAUNTED HOUSE

(On Clifton Hill ☎ 905.357.2200 ext. 6612 🖱 falls.com) Visitors to The Haunted House follow a dark and dreary path while being scared witless by the various ghosts and ghouls contained therein. *($)*

THE FUN HOUSE

(4943 Clifton Hill ☎ 905.357.2200 ext. 6621 🖱 falls.com) Designed mainly for very young children with families, the fun house is a play area with wacky mirrors, a ball-pen, a jail, and a slanted walk-through house. Not very scary, so it is an alternative attraction for those wishing to bypass the area's much more heart-stopping haunted house attractions. *($)*

MYSTERY MAZE

(On Oneida Lane ☎ 905.357.2200 ext. 6067 🖱 falls.com) A little scary and a little twisty, the Mystery Maze is a mini "adventure" where your goal is to find your way through the passageways to one of the small towers. This is a bright and colorful attraction; with a few twists and surprises along the way. *($)*

BRICK CITY

(4943 Clifton Hill ☎ 905.357.2200 ext. 6622 🖱 falls.com) The dome-shaped building at Clifton Hill contains Brick City – a model "city" with replicas of famous area landmarks, made almost entirely with LEGO blocks.

Clifton Hill

Other than looking at a small model town made of LEGO bricks, there is not much to see in Brick City. The tiny electric trains throughout the "town" may thrill the youngest visitors, but a few short minutes of looking is all one really needs to fully experience this attraction. *($)*

CRIMINALS HALL OF FAME

(5751 Victoria Ave. ☎ 905.374.3011) For a more infamous side of Clifton Hill wax museum sect, the Criminals Hall of Fame features criminals that have achieved notorious fame throughout the years. On display are some real criminals at their most infamous moments – such as Jeffrey Dahmer getting a snack from the fridge or Timothy McVeigh in his prison uniform. Others displays are fictitious, such as Hannibal Lecter from *Silence of the Lambs*, or Jason from the *Friday the 13th* movies. This attraction is remotely educational, but mostly scary and a bit intriguing. *($$)*

ARCADES AND AMUSEMENTS

In addition to the walk-through wax museums, Clifton Hill has other amusement attractions and arcades as well. Video and re-demption games, a moving theater, a bowling alley, and even several dark rides and mini-golf courses have prominent homes on this strip.

GREAT CANADIAN MIDWAY

(4912 Clifton Hill ☎ 905.358.3676) Near the foot of Clifton Hill, the Great Canadian Midway has the largest arcade in one of the most substantial indoor amusement centers in the district. From state-of-the-art arcade games and redemption games, combined with 70,000 feet of floor space, the clicking of joysticks, and the loud chatter, this is a true haven for arcade fanatics.

While much of the building houses these arcade games, two other attractions in the facility are worth note: **Ghost Blasters** is a spook-house type dark ride in which guests board a cart equipped with blasters, and they must shoot the targets as they ride through a haunted house (think Disney's Buzz Lightyear's Space Ranger Spin or Universal Orlando's Men in Black ride). For a less interactive experience, the **FX Thrill Ride Theatre** is motion simulator-type "ride" where the seats of the theater move in sync with the action on the large screen.

Outdoors but immediately adjacent to the Great Canadian Midway – just around the corner – is **Dinosaur Park Miniature Golf** (see "Miniature Golf"). Here, guests can enjoy 18 holes in an outdoor scenic dinosaur-themed environment.

FALLSVIEW INDOOR WATERPARK

(Falls Ave. Complex ☎ 800.263.7135 🖱 fallsviewwaterpark.com)
Located on the top floor of the Falls Avenue parking lot (seriously!) this indoor year-round facility is a new gem in the constantly growing array of Clifton Hill attractions. The water-park features 125,000 square feet (and eight stories) of watery fun, including a wave pool, waterslides, a water playground, and video arcade. In summertime, there is a small outdoor pool as well. A small **Planet Hollywood Beach Club** is on-site for quick eats.

While the Fallsview Indoor Waterpark is not a stand-alone resort, it is very easily accessible (via indoor walkways) to many of the Falls Avenue hotels, including the **Sheraton at the Falls, Skyline Inn,** and **Brock Plaza**. It is the perfect family-oriented complement to **Casino Niagara**, which is also accessible through the same building.

NIAGARA SKYWHEEL ✪ Must See!

(4946 Clifton Hill ☎ 905.358.4793) The Niagara SkyWheel is one of the most prominent newer fixtures on Clifton Hill. Visitors can enjoy a rather speedy (and slightly scary) ride around a modern Ferris wheel and at the same time get great views of both the American and Horseshoe Falls. The enclosed climate-controlled cars on the wheel allow for year-round enjoyment without worrying about the "cold air up there." The views, of course are different, depending on the time of day or season. At night, the SkyWheel lights up with the rest of Clifton Hill. It is a landmark and highly visible attraction from all across the falls tourist area. *($)*

ADVENTURE CITY

(4915 Clifton Hill ☎ 905.374.4444) If the Great Canadian Midway is not enough for your arcade and attraction taste, Adventure City is located directly across the street. Here, guests are afforded several ride-type attractions and a smaller collection of arcade games. Bumper cars and an interactive dark ride top the list here.

COSMIC GOLF MINI-GOLF

(On Clifton Hill ☎ 905.358.3676) Play 18 holes of indoor mini-golf set in a weirdly neon space-age, aquatic, interplanetary environment. The lights are blue, and the neon paint glows brightly. *($)*

STRIKE! ROCK N' BOWL

(4912 Clifton Hill ☎ 905.358.4788) Seamlessly attached to the Boston Pizza/Great Canadian Midway complex is a neon-lit "cosmic" (darkly lit, with blue-light effects) bowling alley. The bowling alley features 14 lanes and modern score-keeping computers. Fun for a diversion with friends or family. *($)*

DINOSAUR PARK MINI-GOLF

(On Clifton Hill ☎ 905.358.3676) Behind the Ripley's complex is Dinosaur Park Mini-Golf. The course is 18 holes and can be completed in anywhere from half an hour to several hours (depending on the number of golfers). The theme here is dino-wilderness. Mini-golfers explore the "ancient" Earth, and will run into some pretty scary creatures along the way. (Seasonal) *($)*

FUN EATING AND DRINKING

For visitors looking for some good old-fashioned theme restaurants, they need not look further than right here, the glitzy and kitschy Clifton Hill Entertainment District. This section lists only Clifton Hill restaurants. For the more formal eateries, see the "Select Restaurants" section.

BEER GARDEN

(On Clifton Hill ☎ 905.357.2200 Ext. 1111 🖱 falls.com) Don't let the name dissuade you – this is a great spot for families, adults, and singles alike to gather and relax; and it is literally right in the middle of all that noisy, glorious Clifton Hill action.

The Beer Garden itself is not impressive; it's the location, atmosphere, and clientele that make this one of the most accessible and unique locations at the falls. Located next to the **Thriftlodge** parking lot, this seasonal outdoor patio bar/restaurant is also Niagara's largest karaoke bar. Until the wee hours of the morning (in Niagara talk this is 1:00 or 2.00 a.m. during peak times), pop music blasts while people of all ages sing their favorite songs. People from ages five to 80 jump onto the stage to enthusiastically belt out pop tunes. And what's more fun, their performances are broadcast on closed-circuit television around Clifton Hill. If you're on stage, hundreds – perhaps thousands – of people, are hearing you! As you traverse the area, you are sure to pass this impossible-to-miss attraction – just follow the spotlights. (Outdoor patio seasonal) *($)*

PLANET HOLLYWOOD

(4608 Bender ☎ 905.374.8332 🖱 planethollywood.com) Though the area's Planet Hollywood is not exactly on the strip, it is only a mere seconds away by car (or a bit of an out-of-the-way walk), close to **Casino Niagara**. Here, you can dine alongside famous movie memorabilia, from adventure/science fiction to many others. Or for visitors who'd prefer just a drink, there is a bar area as well.

For such a well-known company, there are fewer Planet Hollywood restaurants than the casual tourist would think – only five in the United States (Honolulu, Las Vegas, Myrtle Beach, New York City, and Downtown Disney in Orlando). However, the chain is all over the world, including Guam, Toronto, Cancun, Bali, and Acapulco. The corporate headquarters is in Orlando. *($$)*

Clifton Hill

HARD ROCK CAFÉ

(5701 Falls Ave. ☎ 905.356.7625 🖱 hardrockcafe.com) The
Hard Rock Café is not located directly on the strip, but rather
a few steps off it, near the foot of Clifton Hill. In addition to
dining amongst famous pieces of music memorabilia (not just
hard rock – much of popular music is represented here), the
restaurant features a rather long 80-foot guitar-shaped bar.

Started by Isaac Tigrett and Peter Morton, the first Hard Rock
Café opened its doors in London, England, in 1971. In the
early 1980s, they began their global expansion. Today, there are
over 120 Hard Rock Café restaurants all over the world.

RAINFOREST CAFÉ

(5685 Falls Ave. ☎ 905.374.2233 🖱 rainforestcafe.com) Though
the Rainforest Café is not officially on Clifton Hill, it can be
accessed via a thru-way near the **MGM Store**. When visitors
enter (either via Clifton Hill or through the volcano-shaped
main entrance), they are transported into a dense jungle,
complete with (robotic) chirping birds, water, and of course,
dense foliage. Every so often, there is a simulated storm in
the restaurant – there is lighting, simulated rain patter, and the
animals even react to the storm.

There are a few dozen Rainforest Café restaurants scattered
around the United States and a few international locations
(including Niagara Falls). There is a Rainforest Café in all
Disney resorts in the United States (two in Orlando), as well as
Disneyland Paris and Tokyo. Landry's Restaurants, Inc. owns
the Rainforest Café chain. The company owns many other
famous (and semi-famous) specialty restaurant chains. *($$)*

T.G.I. FRIDAYS

(#1: 9490 Victoria Ave. ☎ 905.357.4774; #2: 6700 Fallsview Blvd. ☎ 905.356.8523) Thank goodness, it's Friday! There are two T.G.I. Fridays in Niagara Falls. The closest one to Clifton Hill is on Victoria Avenue. This classic family restaurant is great for just an old-fashioned good time.

The first T.G.I. Fridays opened in 1965 in New York City. From this small beginning, the chain has sprung up today to have more than 850 locations. *($$)*

KELSEY'S RESTAURANT

(4960 Clifton Hill ☎ 905.353.0051 🖱 kelseys.ca) Located directly on Clifton Hill is Kelsey's Restaurant. Kelsey's is a mainly Canadian restaurant chain with locations throughout Canada (and one in New York State). They serve a variety of comfort foods in a more laidback family environment. Food includes burgers, pasta, and chicken, all soaking in sauces. *($$)*

RUBY TUESDAY

(On Clifton Hill ☎ 905.357.4330 🖱 rubytuesday.com) Also directly on Clifton Hill, the resident Ruby Tuesday offers outdoor dining patios in seasonally favorable weather, where diners may be able to get a peek of part of the distant American Falls – or watch the action on the street below them. *($$)*

DAVE AND BUSTER'S

(4955 Clifton Hill ☎ 905.371.1331 🖱 daveandbustersniagarafalls.com) Dave and Buster's is half-restaurant and half video arcade. The lower levels are devoted almost entirely to arcade and redemption games, and the upper floors, including a balcony, have a bar and restaurant. The food here is greasy and average – the real draw is the arcade. *($$/$$$)*

SHOPPING

Clifton Hill is the ultimate trinket shop destination. If it's a useless souvenir, then it probably can be bought in one of the shops on Clifton Hill.

THE MARKETPLACE

(On Clifton Hill) The Niagara Falls Marketplace is a true souvenir gift shop – and a rather large one at that. In fact, it is the most substantial gift shop in the Clifton Hill area. The shop features a variety of Niagara Falls and Canadian themed trinkets, shirts, maple candy, souvenir glasses, and much more.

THE FUN FACTORY

(4943 Clifton Hill ☎ 800.263.2557) The Fun Factory is a toy store with a nice collection of unique toys – some for kids, others for all ages. It is crammed with all sorts of things and is definitely worth a look.

MGM STUDIO EXPERIENCE

(Clifton Hill) The MGM Store is adjacent to the nearby **Adventure City** complex. Here, you can buy various pieces of MGM merchandise, including movies/DVDs and collectibles. There are very few (if any other) MGM Stores like this, so it is a unique treat for fans of the company.

Clifton Hill

HERSHEY'S STORE

(5685 Falls Ave. ☎ 905.374.4444 ☻ hersheys.com) For that Niagara Falls sweet tooth, check out the Hershey's Store. At about 7,000 square feet, this is one of the largest chocolate-based retail stores in America. It is located on Falls Avenue, just off Clifton Hill.

Hershey has taken something as simple as chocolate and turned it into an entire commercial culture. Considering the chocolate bar, the theme park, and the chocolate stores, curious folk can see the magic in corporate synergy and branding.

WWE RETAIL STORE

(On Clifton Hill ☎ 905.354.7526 ☻ wwe.com) For wrestling fans, World Wrestling Entertainment has a WWE Retail Store right on Clifton Hill. Here, shoppers may purchase WWE paraphernalia, play Royal Rumble video games, watch Pay-Per-View (for free!), and even experience the **PileDriver** ride – visitors are strapped in, shot up 200 feet, and then dropped down. The facility is large; two floors full of activity. In some aspects, it is more than a store – but it is primarily a store.

FANTASY FUDGE FACTORY

(4960 Clifton Hill) Fantasy Fudge Factory is a nice candy store where they make some kinds of sweets right on the premises as visitors watch. It is a sweet way to spend money.

NIGHTLIFE

For those that prefer to spend the day away from Clifton Hill, don't worry – many of the attractions on Clifton Hill are open late. Depending on the season, some attractions may be open until midnight or later. There are clear advantages to visiting Clifton Hill past dark.

For starters, is a unique experience to see all the signs illuminated in all their glory – lighting the sidewalks and the buildings. Plus, the younger sect of traveler (families with young children) is less abundant, so the crowd creates a bit more of a ruckus.

RUMORS NIGHT CLUB

(4960 Clifton Hill ☎ 905.358.6152 ⬤ rumorsnightclub.com) The Rumors Night Club, located near the top of the Clifton Hill Strip, is one of the most popular nightclubs in the region. It is wired with a state-of-the-art sound system and a D.J. spinning all kinds of dance music. The dance floor itself is large and regularly crowded. There is a mix of tourists and locals, which varies depending on the time of year. Its unique location in a family-oriented tourist area makes for an interesting group of clientele. And when visitors are done dancing, chances are many of the attractions on Clifton Hill may still be open! The club is open year-round, but with reduced days and hours during off season.

HARD ROCK CLUB

(5685 Falls Ave. ☎ 905.356.7625) Part of the **Hard Rock Café** complex within the Falls Avenue building, the Hard Rock Club is where the night owls go who want to drink and dance a bit. Essentially a bar with a dance floor, the club has a high-tech sound system and – it claims – the world's largest electronic disco ball.

Clifton Hill

GREG FREWIN THEATRE

(5781 Ellen Ave. ☎ 905.356.0777 🖱 gregfrewintheatre.com) The newest show to hit the streets of Clifton Hill is pure magic – literally. If you think you'd need to go to Las Vegas to see a wonderfully cheesy magic act, complete with dancers, dramatic music, and exotic animals, think again. The Greg Frewin Theatre tries to emulate Las Vegas shows, with a nice degree of success.

Greg Frewin is a magician, and this theater is built around his magic act, like resident performers of Las Vegas. Though the theater can be used for many types of events, his **Las Vegas Magic Review** show is the dominating force on their calendar. There is also an Elvis tribute, which undoubtedly gives Mr. Frewin the night off. The show holds about 700 audience members. The whole building has a magic theme, with a magical restaurant and a magical bar.

The theater has the layout of a Las Vegas dinner show – you'd be hard-pressed to tell the difference. Visitors may opt for dinner and show or just the show. Dinner is pay-one-price for your choice of various entrées and desserts. *($$$/$$$$)*

Getting Married

Though the vast array of amusements and thrilling attractions in the falls area might give the impression that the whole place is one big theme park, make no mistake – Niagara Falls lives to be romantic. A honeymoon and wedding wonderland since the 1950s, Niagara Falls (in both New York and Ontario) gives out thousands of licenses a year. Plus, when considering that same-sex marriages are legal in Ontario, Niagara Falls has become one of the real "in" places to tie the knot.

GETTING A MARRIAGE LICENSE

Getting a marriage license in Niagara Falls is just a matter of having the right people with the right paperwork go into the right office. Whether obtaining the license in Ontario or New York, it is a good idea to have the following pieces of documentation: (1) a birth certificate and passport for each member of the party, and (2) a certificate of divorce if either party has been married before. There may be minimum age requirements, waiting periods, and ceremonial requirements. Also, depending on where you get the license and perform the ceremony, certain restrictions and requirements may apply. Contact the appropriate city department for more information.

... IN NEW YORK

For licenses granted in New York State, contact the Niagara Falls City Clerk's Office (☎ *716.286.4396*). The office is located at 745 Main Street, room 114. Additional information about New York State marriage licenses can be found online (🖱 *niagarafallsusa.org/ clerk_licenses.html*).

... IN ONTARIO

For licenses granted in Ontario, contact the Niagara Falls City Clerk's Office in City Hall (☎ *905.356.7521*). City Hall is located at 4310 Queen Street. More information about Ontario marriage licenses can be found online (*niagarafalls.ca*).

CEREMONIES

There are many places across the Niagara region that can play host to the wedding of your dreams.

NIAGARA PARKS

(☎ 877.642.7275 niagaraparks.com/aboutus/wedding.php)
It is hard to imagine a wedding ceremony in Niagara Falls without imagining a picturesque garden or a roaring waterfall in the distance. It is for this reason that the Niagara Parks Commission offers some of the best ceremonial environments in Canada. Indoor and outdoor ceremonial areas are available for weddings, including the historic indoor **Queenston Chapel** and beautiful outdoor **Oakes Garden Theatre**. Niagara Parks may provide additional services for ceremonies, including catering and tent/chair rentals. The Niagara Parks also has reception venues, photography services, and more. Contact the Niagara Parks for information.

NIAGARA FALLSVIEW CASINO

(6380 Fallview Blvd. ☎ 866.789.8697
 fallsviewcasinoresort.com) There is a wedding chapel in the Fallsview Casino. In Canada, unlike the United States, a casino wedding chapel is hard to come by. Fallsview, in fact, has a small chapel and a large chapel and can accommodate up to 50

guests for the wedding ceremony. Packages are available and outdoor weddings can also be arranged through the resort.

HONEYMOONS

Of course, you don't have to get married in Niagara Falls to experience its romantic glory – Niagara Falls is also a major honeymoon destination. There are many kinds of honeymoon experiences in the region. A popular place to stay for honeymooners is in one of the fallsview rooms of the **Fallsview** section of town. For popular romantic activities, see the Top Romantic Activities in the "Recommendations" section of this book.

On the northern tip of the Niagara River, Niagara-on-the-Lake is frequently cited as one of the prettiest small towns in North America.

Greater Niagara Region

●

The Niagara Peninsula on the Canadian side is a major vacation area even beyond that of Niagara Falls. Natural landscapes, wineries, adventures, quaint towns, and much more are in this area. Lake Erie and Lake Ontario border the peninsula on the north and south and the Niagara River on the east. Visitors vacationing in the greater Niagara region may never need to see the falls – it is a much quieter and more peaceful vacationing experience.

This section focuses on some general interest material in this region. For more specific information or more specific touring tips, contact addition resources or visit the **Tourism Niagara** Web site (● *tourismniagara.com)*. Though 12 million of the more than 18 million visitors come only to see the falls, those that venture away from the Niagara River find many pleasant surprises.

NIAGARA-ON-THE-LAKE ✪ Must See!

([*] Greater Niagara Region ● niagaraonthelake.com) On the Niagara River at Lake Ontario (due north of Niagara Falls) is one of the prettiest small towns in North America. This spot is internationally acclaimed for its restaurants, theater, cultural activities, and much more. Any overnight visit to Niagara Falls deserves a quick 15-mile jaunt up to this paradise. With so many perfect picture-taking opportunities, Niagara-on-the-Lake is world renowned for its artistic community. From theater to art galleries to music, this is the place to behold some of Canada's greatest works. Attractions here include the famous **Shaw Festival** (☎ *905.468.2153* ● *shawfest.com)*, a theater company with a regular schedule of performances. Named for Bernard Shaw, the festival highlights plays and productions from Oscar Wilde, Chekhov, and more. A season runs from April through December.

There are so, so many art galleries – comparable in quantity to New York City's SoHo but in a much quainter environment. From paintings to sculptures to almost every conceivable form of visual art, it can all be found here. Listings for some of these galleries may be found at the Niagara-on-the-Lake Web site.

FORT GEORGE

(🍁 **26 Queen St., Niagara-on-the-Lake, ON ☎ 905.468.4257 🖱 pc.gc.ca)** On the Canadian side, Fort George protected British interests and was the British Army's Centre Division headquarters during the War of 1812. The fort is located directly across the river from New York State's **Fort Niagara**. Fort George was created directly in military response to Fort Niagara. It was largely destroyed by American attacks in 1813 ("the Battle of Fort George"). It was later rebuilt but eventually abandoned for better locations.

Today visitors are allowed to explore the fort and the various buildings. The fort is where General Sir Isaac Brock served his final military duty. The hours are seasonal, so call in advance for more information. *($/$$)*

FORT ERIE

(🍁 **Greater Niagara Region ☎ 905.871.0540 🖱 forteriecanada.com)** Located at the southern tip of the Niagara River at Lake Erie, Fort Erie was established as a military site by the British in 1764 due to its strategic location to protect the north-flowing Niagara River. Today it is the closest Canadian city to Buffalo, and visitors from Buffalo take the Peace Bridge directly into Fort Erie.

The main historical attraction here is of course Fort Erie itself. Much fighting was done at Fort Erie during the War of 1812, and the museum stands today as a memorial as well as a place to learn. *($/$$)*

OLD FORT NIAGARA
(▭ **Youngstown, NY** ☎ **716.745.7611** ⚲ **oldfortniagara.org**) On the American side, Old Fort Niagara is a National Historic Landmark and about 300 years old. The fort is a collection of fortified buildings with varying defense-related histories – the first was built in 1674. In the 1700s, the French used it in part to protect "New France" during the French and Indian War. It changed hands several times – between the French, Americans, and finally the British (during the War of 1812).

Today, the site is preserved as it was during the 1700s, and visitors may tour some of the facilities year-round. Historical recreations of important events also occur regularly at the fort. *($/$$)*

WINE COUNTRY

The vineyards of the northeast – New Jersey, upstate New York, and others, aren't as well known as the wine country of California. However, the Niagara Peninsula has much more than its share of vineyards. Visitors wanting a tour of wine-making facilities, or free wine tasting, or any number of wine-oriented activities, needn't look far from Niagara Falls. There are literally dozens of vineyards in the region, and many of them are situated near **Niagara-on-the-Lake**. But for the truly remote vineyard experience, consider trekking west – beyond the well-populated Niagara River area, and into the true heart of the Niagara Peninsula.

Following is a list of popular vineyards and wineries of the greater Niagara region. As each winery/vineyard experience is different, it is recommended that visitors contact the establishments beforehand. Also, vineyards are generally seasonal attractions, however certain facilities (such as gift shops on premises) may be open during the winter.

CHÂTEAU DES CHARMES

(1025 York Rd., Sr. David's, ON ☎ 800.263.2541
☗ chateaudescharmes.com) Tours of the vineyard are offered regularly, and wine tasting is available. Wines may be purchased online or on-site.

HENRY OF PELHAM FAMILY ESTATE WINERY

(1469 Pelham Rd., St. Catharines, ON ☎ 905.684.8423
☗ henryofpelham.com) Facility tours and wine tasting are offered. The on-site **Coach House Café** specializes in cheese. Also on-site is an art gallery that showcases Canadian artists.

HERNDER ESTATE WINES

(1607 Eighth Ave., St. Catharines, ON ☎ 905.684.3300
☗ hernder.com) The vineyard offers tours and wine tasting. Customers may also order wines online through their **Wine Club**. Hernder also provides facilities for weddings and other special events.

HILLEBRAND ESTATES WINERY

(12459 Niagara Stone Rd., Niagara-on-the-Lake, ON
☎ 905.468.7123 🖰 hillebrand.com) Tours of the facilities and
wine tasting is available. Hillerbrand sells wines on their Web
site and via a **Wine Club**. The on-site restaurant offers a
variety of wines and food.

INNISKILLIN WINES

(R.R. #1, Line 3, Niagara-on-the-Lake, ON ☎ 888.466.4754
🖰 inniskillin.com) Tours and wine tasting are scheduled regularly.

JACKSON-TRIGGS NIAGARA ESTATE WINERY

(2145 R. R. #55, Niagara-on-the-Lake, ON ☎ 905.468.4637
🖰 jacksontriggswinery.com) Tours and wine tasting are regularly
scheduled. Jackson-Triggs also has event space available.

JOSEPH'S ESTATE WINES

(1811 Niagara Stone Rd., Niagara-on-the-Lake, ON
☎ 905.468.1259 🖰 josephsestatewines.com) Joseph's offers
tours of the vineyard and facilities, and wine tasting on-site.

MAGNOTTA WINERY

(271 Chrislea Rd., Vaughan, ON ☎ 905.738.9463
🖰 magnotta.com) Tours and tasting sessions are regularly scheduled. Magnotta has a retail store and products are also available
online.

PELLER ESTATES WINERY

(290 John St., Niagara-on-the-Lake, ON ☎ 905.468.4678
🖰 peller.com) Tours and wine tasting are available. There is an
on-site restaurant. Wines can be purchased online.

REIF WINERY

**(15608 Niagara Parkway, Niagara-on-the-Lake, ON
☎ 905.468.7738 ♟ reifwinery.com)** Wine tasting and tours are available. Wines may be purchased online or via their Wine Club. Facilities for weddings and other events are available.

OTHER CITIES

The Niagara region has several major metropolitan areas within close driving distance, both within Ontario and New York State. What follows are complete destinations in and of themselves – they warrant a separate trip to be fully appreciated.

TORONTO

Toronto is the most populous city in Canada, and a major economic powerhouse. It is everything you'd expect a major city to be – a center for commerce, arts, entertainment, tourism, development, and politics. In fact, 23 percent of the population of Canada lives in and around Toronto. The area surrounding Toronto and bordered by the Great Lakes is called the Golden Horseshoe (which includes Niagara Falls), and the area is fed largely by Toronto. Like New York City, Tokyo, and Paris, Toronto is a major world city.

Many people like to compare Toronto to New York City, sometimes calling it "Little New York." While it is true that both cities mark the urban apex of their respective countries, there are marked differences between the two metropolises. Toronto is smaller with about three million residents within the city proper (NYC has eight million). It's also cleaner, a bit more relaxed, and a bit more liberal with the arts (Canada's government has special enticements to attract the art community to this city). Portions of Toronto have been used to emulate other major cities – such as New York – in many feature films.

The **Canada's National Tower** (or CN Tower) is always a highlight attraction for first-time visitors. At over 1,800 feet, it is the tallest "building" in the world. Also here is the **Toronto Zoo** (☎ *416.392.5900)*, the **Art Gallery of Ontario** (☎ *416.979.6648)*, and the **Casa Loma** (☎ *416.923.1171)* historic site.

There are many travel books on Toronto – and they regularly include information on Niagara Falls. But if you're wishing to explore Toronto, although it is only 90 miles away, is not a one-day excursion; there are simply too many great things to do.

BUFFALO

New York's largest city in the greater Niagara region is much closer to Niagara Falls than the largest city on the Canadian side. In fact, the Peace Bridge from downtown Buffalo takes visitors over the Niagara River and right into **Fort Erie**. Buffalo closely associates itself with the Niagara region – even the airport is called "Buffalo Niagara" and the public transportation system is called "Niagara Frontier." The city is bordered by the Niagara River and Lake Erie.

Buffalo is considered part of the "Buffalo Niagara" region, and as such the city proper promotes the Niagara region's many attractions. For many touring the region, Buffalo serves as the gateway to Niagara. It has the closest large airport, and very easy access to Canada. As a small city, however, Buffalo has some treats that deserve a second look. Buffalo winters are famous – it snows an average of 180 inches each year, and many people come during this time to partake in wintertime activities. And yes: in 1964, Buffalo Wings were invented here.

Recommendations

Following is a quick listing of the top attractions of various categories, including food, family attractions, and romantic attractions. The lists include (when applicable) addresses, phone numbers, and other pertinent information to help your travels get up and running as quickly as possible. If you need more information about one of the attractions on the following pages, simply find that attraction's detailed listing elsewhere in the book.

TOP FAMILY ATTRACTIONS

In a nutshell, following is a brief summary of the top family attractions as determined by the author, including basic family-oriented information, as well as an address and phone number (when applicable). For more detailed information, see the full attraction listing elsewhere in this book.

BUTTERFLY CONSERVATORY

(2405 Niagara Pkwy. ☎ 905.358.0025) Walk around an interior greenhouse filled to the brim with all kinds of butterflies. Great family attraction; butterflies will probably land on you.

GREAT CANADIAN MIDWAY

(4912 Clifton Hill ☎ 905.358.3676) Huge video arcade with rides and other attractions. Loud and noisy; older kids and teens will love it and never ever want to leave.

GREG FREWIN DINNER THEATRE

(5781 Ellen Ave. ☎ 905.356.0777) Las Vegas-style magic acts and other shows. Nicely produced, family-friendly dinner show.

JOURNEY BEHIND THE FALLS

(6650 Niagara Pkwy. ☎ 905.354.1551) An easy elevator ride and walk to view the back of the falls. The long caves underground are a bit dark and claustrophobic.

MAID OF THE MIST

(5920 Niagara Pkwy. ☎ 905.358.0311) Thrilling soaking-wet boat ride up to the foot of Horseshoe Falls. Young children might be scared, since the boat rocks and the falls are loud.

MARINELAND

(7657 Portage Rd. ☎ 905.356.9565) Aquatic-centered amusement theme park. Lots to do (and even lots more walking) for younger children.

NIAGARA FALLS AVIARY

(5651 River Rd. ☎ 905.356.8888) A huge indoor tropical environment with all kinds of exotic birds. Great family attraction.

NIAGARA FALLS STATE PARK

Large park with plenty of walking paths and great views of the American Falls and Canada. Also on-property are lots of falls-based attractions, such as **Cave of the Winds** and the American rapids.

RIPLEY'S BELIEVE IT OR NOT! MUSEUM

(4983 Clifton Hill ☎ 905.356.2238) Walk-through wax museum filled with oddities. Kind of dark, spooky, and some of the exhibits are a bit unpleasant. Older children only.

SKYLON TOWER

(5200 Robinson St. ☎ 905.356.2651) Very interesting center with a great view of the falls and glass elevators zooming visitors to the top. Might frighten those who are scared of heights.

TABLE ROCK POINT

(650 Niagara Pkwy.) Complex with shopping, eating, and excellent Horseshoe Falls views. One of the easiest places to see the falls and view the falls' illumination at night.

WHIRLPOOL AERO CAR

(3850 Niagara Pkwy. ☎ 905.354.5711) Dangle over the Whirlpool Rapids in a gondola-style hanging contraption. Not recommended for anyone even a little bit scared of heights.

TOP ROMANTIC ACTIVITIES

Romance is always in the air at Niagara Falls, and here are a few things couples can do to enjoy their time at this romantic getaway (aside from getting married, of course!).

HELICOPTER RIDES

(See "The Falls from the Air") An experience you can share with your significant other forever.

MAID OF THE MIST

(5920 Niagara Pkwy. ☎ 905.358.0311) You can't beat this; possibly the most romantic boat ride ever.

NIAGARA FALLSVIEW CASINO

(6380 Fallsview Blvd. ☎ 888.FALLSVUE) Enjoy slots and table games, walk the shopping promenade, or just relax at one of the many bars and restaurants.

NIAGARA GRAND DINNER THEATRE

(8444 Lundy's Lane ☎ 905.357.7818) The shows are romantic and comical; the dinners add a unique touch.

NIAGARA-ON-THE-LAKE

(North of Niagara Falls) Beautiful small town; perfect for strolling, enjoying art galleries, and shopping.

QUEEN VICTORIA PARK

Take a nice stroll through this riverside park, and you'll see why many people choose to exchange vows here.

RAINBOW BRIDGE WALKING

Across this bridge offers great views of both the falls illumination and fireworks.

SKYLON TOWER

(5200 Robinson St. ☎ 905.356.2651) View the falls from atop one of the tallest structures in the Niagara region.

VINEYARD TOURS

(See "Wine Country") Many of the vineyards in the Niagara region offer wine tasting and tours.

TRAVEL SCENARIOS

Following are vacation possibilities under various circumstances. Though Niagara Falls vacations are generally very flexible, to experience some attractions you may need to plan in advance. Information about the specific attractions within these travel scenarios can be found elsewhere in this book.

JUST A GLIMPSE

(*Time:* Half a day, or less; *When to go:* Anytime) Niagara Falls has the advantage of being a totally flexible destination. While you could spend many days at all the attractions, the falls themselves are there to be looked at for any amount of time. The nearby cities of Toronto, Hamilton, Buffalo, and other points within the Niagara region regularly feed visitors to the falls, who merely want a glimpse of this awe-inspiring wonder. They drive up to **Table Rock Point** (Ontario) or the **Niagara Falls State Park** (New York), spend a few minutes gawking, and then are off on their merry way. There is no admission fee to see the falls and there are many public access points – though many of the area parking spots require payment.

Recommendations: Arrive anytime, day or night. During the day, the falls are spectacular as usual. At night, when the sun is down, the falls are illuminated with bright colorful lights in many directions. The illumination isn't constant, so if you intend to arrive at the falls just to see the illumination (or fireworks), contact the Niagara Parks Commission in advance.

THE FALLS UP CLOSE

(*Time:* Full Day; *When to Go:* Summer Daytime) For those who want a little bit more of a tour than simply looking over the

Great Gorge, the Niagara Parks Commission has many attractions that allow you to explore the falls in a closer, sometimes more thrilling way, but that require a bit more of your time. The most famous and popular attraction of course is **Maid of the Mist**, which brings visitors literally into the mouth of Horseshoe Falls by boat. Most one-day excursions to the falls in the summertime will encompass a Maid of the Mist voyage. If you are visiting in the wintertime, you will be limited in your possibilities (Maid of the Mist is closed in winter). However, another top-notch attraction is **Journey Behind the Falls**, which is open year-round (on a limited basis in the winter).

Recommendations: Arrive in the morning – definitely before noon. The falls-exploring attractions are generally only open during the daytime in the summer, and at peak season the tickets for the day sell out fast.

CASINO VACATION

(*Time:* Half Day to Full Day; *When to Go:* Anytime) The immediate Niagara Falls area is home to three casinos – two on the Ontario side and one in New York. Though there are limited accommodations on the premises of certain casinos for spending the night, many more people just come to gamble, and either take their accommodation needs elsewhere, or head back home.

Recommendations: The casinos are all open 24 hours, and they are all enclosed, so there is no need to arrive at a specific day or time – there will always be available action on the casino floor. The **Niagara Fallsview Casino** is the most complete gaming facility in Niagara Falls (it has resort amenities), but **Casino Niagara** is closer to Clifton Hill. The **Seneca Niagara Casino** is right across the river in New York.

ROMANTIC WEEKEND

(*Time:* 1 Night; *When to Go:* Summertime) For a quick romantic getaway, there is no better place than Niagara Falls. With so many large resorts, suites, elegant restaurants, peaceful parks and gardens, and the roaring Niagara River, you and your loved one will be among the thousands of couples coming to the falls each year to cherish their love for each other. Weddings and honeymoons occur here all the time. If this is what you're after, book well in advance and consult a professional wedding or honeymoon coordinator.

Recommendations: Romantic trips to the falls must be planned in advance – you want the best suite at the cheapest price, reservations at a top restaurant, and perhaps tickets for one of the local shows. Stay at one of the larger resorts in the Fallsview section of town, which are all close to the **Fallsview Casino** and overlook Horseshoe Falls. (Plan carefully: some resorts in this section are smaller. Choosing a name-brand, high-end resort such as **Hilton** or **Sheraton Fallsview** might be your best bet). Ask if they have a "fallsview" room and any levels of suites.

During the day, stroll through **Queen Victoria Park**, and check out the **Niagara Falls Aviary** – the exotic birds are very interesting, and the indoor environment is beautiful. For a romantic dinner, dine around **Table Rock Point** or right in your resort (several of them have upper-crust restaurants on or near the top floor with great views). If you would like a more subdued environment for strolling or eating, the nearby **Niagara-on-the-Lake** is one of the prettiest towns in North America, and it is filled with artistic pleasures and fine eateries.

FAMILY WEEKEND

(*Time:* 2 Nights; *When to Go:* Summertime) Niagara Falls is perfect for families! Not only is there a sheer diversity of attractions for all age levels, many of them can be enjoyed by everybody, parents and kids alike. From the adventuresome falls themselves to the quieter parks to the roaring amusement sections, everybody will find something. Two nights is not enough time to do everything – but vacations with the family here can be hectic, and there's no need to do everything.

Recommendations: Definitely arrive as early as possible. Even before checking into your hotel, head over to **Table Rock Point** and admire the falls first-hand. Then head over to the **Maid of the Mist** dock and secure tickets for an afternoon boat ride – do this *first* – it is the best attraction in Niagara Falls.

Kids and young adults will likely want to visit Clifton Hill right away as it is home to all sorts of diversions. Pre-dominantly an older kids' spot, it's a great place for arcades, rides, and other such amusement-y things. It is a bit of a rough crowd, so younger children should not be left unsupervised. The area's wax museums and haunted houses are for big kids as well – and many adults will find Ripley's very entertaining. Clifton Hill is best in the evening or at night, so after introduction to Niagara Falls and your **Maid of the Mist** voyage, Clifton Hill is a good place to head for dinner.

Which hotel is best for families? The range is across the board. There are a few motel-style good choices directly on Clifton Hill which can get a little loud at night with the outside commotion. The Fallsview section has the larger upscale resorts, so depending on your family's needs, either of those two places would be best. Try to avoid a less populous or touristy section of town, as the area may not be as safe.

For the full day, plan on one of the day-enveloping activities of the area. There are at least three area theme parks here. Don't try to hit them all on this trip. Just pick the one that looks most suited to your family's liking and spend the day there. Families may also enjoy time at the **Butterfly Conservatory** or the **Niagara Falls Aviary** – both very popular attractions. Your family may also enjoy the Whirlpool Rapids. The **Whirlpool Aero Car** is a bit scary for the young ones, but it is very thrilling. For an unusual look at Horseshoe Falls, the **Journey Behind the Falls** attraction at **Table Rock Point** is very unique. To wrap up the busy day, spend the evening again at Clifton Hill.

THRILL-SEEKERS WEEKEND

(*Time:* **1 or 2 Nights;** *When to Go:* **Summertime**) You don't need to be a daredevil at Niagara Falls to enjoy some truly thrilling experiences. There are several ways to see the falls and river that are much more than just "looking" – experience the thrill.

Maid of the Mist may be family-oriented, but it is also rather thrilling. Guests board a small boat and head into the mouth of Horseshoe Falls. Be prepared to get soaked and rocked around a bit by the current. To get even closer to the base of the falls, the **Cave of the Winds** takes visitor up to about 20 feet from Bridal Veil Falls. From here, the wind, the mist, and the intensity are amazing. Guests are given special shoes to wear as they make the descent into the Great Gorge and along the platform to the base of the falls.

A short trip north to **Niagara-on-the-Lake** offers thrill-seekers the chance to actually brave the dangerous whirlpool and rapids first-hand with the Whirlpool Jet Boat Tours, which twists and turns for 18 miles at speeds of up to 65 per hour. It's a soaking rush on some of the world's most dangerous rapids.

COLLEGE GETAWAY

(*Time:* 1 Evening; *When to Go:* Anytime) The gambling and drinking age in Ontario is 19. For many college-aged folk, this is reason enough to cross the border and enjoy the fruits of Canada. In Niagara Falls, less than a mile from the Rainbow Bridge is not one, but two full-fledged casinos. In addition, Clifton Hill offers more bars and restaurants than anyone could reasonably visit in a week. **Casino Niagara** is right in the Clifton Hill area too, so an evening of fun for young and almost-old alike.

It is common for students visiting from Buffalo to spend the evening in Niagara Falls – the bar scene hops until about 2:00 a.m. on busy summer weekends. Nightclubs such as **Rumours** are in full swing during peak weekend periods as well.

THE FULL NIAGARA FALLS EXPERIENCE

(*Time:* 3 Nights; *When to Go:* Summertime) For those wishing to experience all that Niagara Falls has to offer, consider a vacation of about three nights and two full days. While it is possible to putter around for weeks, eating and drinking, and exploring the many parks, a solid three days will give visitors enough time to hit all the attractions, explore the surroundings, see the falls from as many angles as modern science will allow, and still have leisure time left over. Scheduling a visit to all the "must-see" attractions located throughout this book will give visitors the full Niagara Falls experience.

AUTHOR'S RECOMMENDATIONS

Here, I (the author) get to tell you my favorite attractions, things to do, places to go, itineraries, and whatever else catches my fancy. The information here is *personal*. What do I like to do? What are my favorite attractions, hotels, restaurants, etc.?

I am happy that there is a tourist town like Niagara Falls. After writing about such adult-themed locations as Atlantic City, where the main focus is gambling, drinking, and other such endeavors, writing about Niagara Falls is indeed a pleasure. This is a place so diverse and splendid that many different kinds of vacations are possible – adults can have fun, children can have fun, couples can have fun, and even singles can have fun.

WHEN TO GO

Wintertime at the falls is much less expensive, and the crowds are greatly diminished. This is no surprise, as many of the key attractions don't operate off season. However, some of them do, and wintertime can often be a great experience – especially for romantic couples who merely want to spend time together.

However, nothing beats a summertime romp through this watery wonderland. When the crowds come out and the heat rises, all the best of Niagara is there to behold! The flowers and trees are in full bloom, the attractions are active, and the falls themselves are as beautiful as ever.

ACCOMMODATIONS

I always stay on the Canadian side of the falls. When I want a romantic vacation, I definitely prefer one of the Fallsview resorts; particularly the **Fallsview Casino Resort** or the **Hilton**. The two resorts are right next to each other, and are right near the middle of the Fallsview section of town.

Sometimes, however, I want to be near the fun zone – Clifton Hill. In this case, I prefer to stay at one of the noisiest hotels in Niagara Falls – the **Travelodge** or **Thriftlodge** right on Clifton Hill. It is just a hop outside to all the Clifton Hill amusement attractions, bars, and restaurants. The **Quality Inn** on the other side of the street offers a similar experience.

As the Fallsview and Clifton Hill hotels are a bit expensive (especially during the summertime), I sometimes opt for the cheaper accommodations at Lundy's Lane. The area is only a short drive from the falls, and even if you don't have a car, the Niagara Transit buses are available to take visitors from these less expensive hotels to the falls and area attractions.

FAVORITE ATTRACTIONS

Maid of the Mist is the first attraction I see. It is especially fantastic on very hot summer days; the misty water from the American and Horseshoe Falls cools me down. When it's *really* hot, I also enjoy the Whirlpool Jet Boat Tours (the "wet jet" boats), since I get soaking wet when crashing into all those rapids.

I enjoy wandering around the **Niagara Falls State Park** and looking at the sights; it is much more woodsy and secluded-feeling than the Canadian side's Niagara Parks Commission.

Plus, I have greater (and closer) access to the American and Bridal Veil Falls. At places I can actually walk right under or next to the falls. **Cave of the Winds** is, in a way, pointless (very little opportunity for learning) but thrilling nonetheless.

Table Rock Point is my favorite place to view Horseshoe Falls. I especially like to walk on the sidewalk (along the Niagara Parkway) between the American Falls/Clifton Hill area to Table Rock. This walk is popular and crowded, so it does take time.

In the wintertime, the casinos and Clifton Hill are the best places to be; Canadian winters are freezing, and these areas feature a variety of year-round indoor attractions.

WEB SITES

There are many sources for additional information regarding Niagara Falls. This book is merely a piece of the literary patchwork that allows those desiring more to learn as much as they want. Following is a list of additional online sources that will fill in the gaps of this publication, as well as provide more accurate and thorough information.

There are some great Internet resources on Niagara Falls. When planning your trip to the falls, these Web sites provide additional information – you may also be able to book hotels and secure tickets online.

CITY OF NIAGARA FALLS

(🖱 www.city.niagarafalls.on.ca) The official Web site to Niagara Falls, Ontario, has information about all kinds of city services, including tourist information, traffic statistics, and even marriage license obtainment.

NIAGARA PARKS COMMISSION

(🖱 niagaraparks.com) A fantastic Web site with in-depth information about the Niagara Parks, including all of the headlining attractions – **Maid of the Mist, Journey Behind the Falls, White Water Walk, Whirlpool Aero Car,** and much more. This is my favorite tourist-centered site – highly recommended.

CLIFTON HILL

(🖱 cliftonhill.com) A major depot of promotional information regarding the attractions, restaurants, and accommodations on and around Clifton Hill. Also learn about the history of Clifton Hill and the area's tourism industry.

TOURISM NIAGARA

(🖱 tourismniagara.com) Web site dedicated to the travel within the greater Niagara region, including Niagara Falls. Though information here is not at first glance substantial, it directs potential visitors to a plethora of other Web sites with more detailed information.

NIAGARA FALLS LIVE

(🖱 niagarafallslive.com) Interesting Web site with information, photos, and descriptions for many of the area's attractions. Site features information about both the American and Canadian sides of the falls.

NIAGARA FALLS THUNDER ALLEY

(🖱 niagarafrontier.com) Comprehensive Web site dedicated to three facets of Niagara Falls: history, tourism, and general information. This site contains a lot of facts and information that don't exist at other more promotional-based Web sites.

U.S. DEPARTMENT OF STATE
CANADA BORDER SERVICES AGENCY

(🖱 travel.state.gov, csba.gc.ca) These official Web sites, for the United States and Canada respectively, discuss border-crossing, customs, and other such information.

Index

Index

Index

Index

NOTES:

NOTES:

NOTES:

NOTES:

NOTES:

°tourist town guides

Explore America's Fun Places

Books in the *Tourist Town Guides*® series are available at bookstores and online. You can also visit our Web site for additional book and travel information. The address is:

http://www.touristtown.com

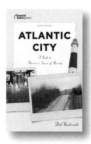

Atlantic City (4th Edition)

This guide will introduce a new facet of Atlantic City that goes beyond the appeal exercised by its lavish casinos. Atlantic City is one of the most popular vacation destinations in the United States.

Price: $14.95; ISBN: 978-1-935455-00-4

Gatlinburg (2nd Edition)

Whether it is to see the weird and wonderful displays at Ripley's Believe It or Not! Museum, or to get the adrenalin pumping with some outdoor activity or to revel in the extravaganza of Dollywood, people come to the Smokies for a variety of reasons – and they are never disappointed!

Price: $14.95; ISBN: 978-1-935455-04-2

Hilton Head

A barrier island off the coast of South Carolina, Hilton Head is a veritable coastal paradise. This destination guide gives a detailed account of this resort island, tailor made for a coastal vacation.

Price: $14.95; ISBN: 978-1-935455-06-6

Myrtle Beach (2nd Edition)

The sunsets are golden and the pace is relaxed at Myrtle Beach, the beachside playground for vacationers looking for their fill of sun, sand, and surf. Head here for the pristine beaches, the shopping opportunities, the sea of attractions, or simply to kick back and unwind.

Price: $14.95; ISBN: 978-1-935455-01-1

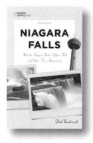

Niagara Falls (3rd Edition)

The spirited descent of the gushing falls may be the lure for you, but in Niagara Falls, it is the smorgasbord of activities and attractions that will keep you coming back for more!

Price: $14.95; ISBN: 978-1-935455-03-5

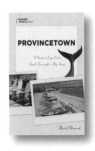

Provincetown

With a rich heritage and proud history, Provincetown is America's oldest art colony, but there is more to this place than its culture. The guide to Provincetown explores its attractions and accommodations, culture and recreation in detail to reveal a vacation destination definitely worth visiting.

Price: $13.95; ISBN: 978-1-935455-07-3

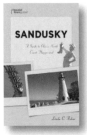

Sandusky

The Cedar Point Amusement Park may be the main reason to visit Sandusky, but this comprehensive guide provides ample reason to stick around and explore Sandusky and the neighboring islands.

Price: $13.95; ISBN: 978-0-9767064-5-8

Williamsburg

The lure to explore history is unmistakable in the town, but Williamsburg is so much more than its rich history. Head to this region to discover the modern facets of this quaint town, indulge in activities guaranteed to hook your interest, and step into the past in this historically significant destination.

Price: $14.95; ISBN: 978-1-935455-05-9

Also Available: (See http://www.touristtown.com for details)

Black Hills	Price: $14.95; ISBN: 978-0-9792043-1-9)
Breckenridge	Price: $14.95; ISBN: 978-0-9767064-9-6)
Frankenmuth	Price: $13.95; ISBN: 978-0-9767064-8-9)
Hershey	Price: $13.95; ISBN: 978-0-9792043-8-8)
Jackson Hole	Price: $13.95; ISBN: 978-0-9792043-3-3)
Key West (2nd Edition)	Price: $14.95; ISBN: 978-1-935455-02-8)
Las Vegas	Price: $13.95; ISBN: 978-0-9792043-5-7)
Mackinac	Price: $14.95; ISBN: 978-0-9767064-7-2)
Ocean City	Price: $13.95; ISBN: 978-0-9767064-6-5)
Wisconsin Dells	Price: $13.95; ISBN: 978-0-9792043-9-5)

www.touristtown.com

ORDER FORM #1
ON REVERSE SIDE

Tourist Town Guides® is published by:
Channel Lake, Inc.
P.O. Box 1771
New York, NY 10156

ORDER FORM

Telephone: With your credit card handy,
call toll-free 800.592.1566

Fax: Send this form toll-free to 866.794.5507

E-mail: Send the information on this form
to orders@channellake.com

Postal mail: Send this form with payment to Channel Lake, Inc.
P.O. Box 1771, New York, NY, 10156

Your Information: ( ) Do not add me to your mailing list

Name: _____

Address: _____

City: _____ State: _____ Zip: _____

Telephone: _____

E-mail: _____

Book Title(s) / ISBN(s) / Quantity / Price
(see previous page or www.touristtown.com for this information)

_____

_____

_____

Total payment*: $_____

Payment Information: (Circle One) Visa / Mastercard

Number: _____ Exp: _____

Or, make check payable to: **Channel Lake, Inc.**

* Add the lesser of $6.50 USD or 18% of the total purchase price for shipping. International orders call or e-mail first! New York orders add 8% sales tax.

www.touristtown.com

ORDER FORM #2
ON REVERSE SIDE

Tourist Town Guides® is published by:
Channel Lake, Inc.
P.O. Box 1771
New York, NY 10156

ORDER FORM

Telephone: With your credit card handy,
call toll-free 800.592.1566

Fax: Send this form toll-free to 866.794.5507

E-mail: Send the information on this form
to orders@channellake.com

Postal mail: Send this form with payment to Channel Lake, Inc.
P.O. Box 1771, New York, NY, 10156

Your Information: ( ) Do not add me to your mailing list

Name: _____

Address: _____

City: _____ State: _____ Zip: _____

Telephone: _____

E-mail: _____

Book Title(s) / ISBN(s) / Quantity / Price
(see previous page or www.touristtown.com for this information)

_____

_____

_____

Total payment*: $_____

Payment Information: (Circle One)   Visa / Mastercard

Number: _____ Exp: _____

Or, make check payable to: **Channel Lake, Inc.**

** Add the lesser of $6.50 USD or 18% of the total purchase price
for shipping. International orders call or e-mail first! New York
orders add 8% sales tax.*